" I can't have a bright outlook to be released under the present government. I think I am now in the period of darkness. But I will endure this darkness well. I will stand this darkness, keeping my health and accomplishing spiritual growth."

—From a letter written by

Prisoner of Conscience Kim Song-Man

September 23, 1995

Enduring the Darkness:
A Story of Conscience, Hope and Triumph

Letters from Kim Song-man, an Amnesty International Prisoner of Conscience in South Korea, 1985 to 15 August 1998

Compiled and edited by Drake Zimmerman

With Ruth Cobb

Amnesty International Adoption Group #202
Normal, Illinois

Amnesty International Adoption Group #202
Normal, Illinois

Enduring the Darkness: A Story of Conscience, Hope and Triumph
Letters from Kim Song-man, an Amnesty International Prisoner of
Conscience in South Korea, 1985 to 15 August 1998

Excerpts from various Amnesty International
publications and letters used with permission

Illustrations from *Composed by Death Row Inmate; Lyrics by
Prisoner of Conscience: A Collection of Prison Letters by
Kim Seong-Man,* by Minkahyup used with permission
(First Edition published by HIM in Seoul, Republic of Korea, 1991)

Ordering information:
Babbitt's Books
104 North Street, Normal, IL USA (309) 454-7393
e-mail: babbitts.books@gte.net
web site: http://www.babbittsbooks.com/

PRICE: $9.95 U.S. — $13.95 Canada
*quantity discounts available—especially for fundraising by
Amnesty International Groups*

ISBN:0-9703359-0-3
Library of Congress Catalog Card Number: 00-135342

We wish to thank Amnesty International's Special Initiatives Fund
for the grant to purchase of copies of this book for use as a training
and fundraising tool for Amnesty groups.

Profits from the sale of this publication will be donated to
Amnesty International

Contents

Acknowledgments

A special thanks to Clare McVey of Amnesty International's East Asian Center in London for tireless and unending help over the years, and to Michael O'Reilly in the AIUSA Atlanta office who gave Adoption Group #202 the case in the first place. Your encouragement kept the case with us when we thought we were not writing enough, and honed the wilder ideas to provide quantities of letters and packages to Kim Song-man.

Thanks also to Ed Baker and Michael Dodd, AI country coordinators, for their many ideas. We are deeply indebted to Choi In-hwa, Kim Song-man's mother, for her steadfast efforts on her son's behalf.

This book would not have been possible without the formatting and graphics help of Todd Bushman of the Dalkey Archive Press. Kristin Hill, Sherry Hill and Adam Silverman added extraordinary editorial comments and organization. Many thanks to Julie Boswell, who typed in innumerable letters. We are also indebted to Steven Monk who kept address labels typed and mailed out over the years. Dr. S.J. Chang of Illinois State University, Normal, Illinois, provided valuable assistance with translation.

Ruth Cobb's editing, formatting and tireless legwork brought this book into being. She brought order and clarity to what we had assembled and serves herself as ongoing inspiration.

Thanks are due to the founders of Adoption Group #202, Normal, Illinois: Judy and Jerry Stone, Jim and Lois Whitehurst, G.L. and Betty Story, Marilea White, Jack Hobbs, N. Grier Hills, Mike Gorr and the many members who have written letters over the years.

Finally, a giant THANK YOU to the Amnesty International staff who carry out the formidable task of encouraging millions of us to write letters on behalf of prisoners around the world. Those letters are beacons of light that make a difference in the world.

Editor's Note

We have tried to make this collection of letters and materials relating to this Amnesty International case as informative and meaningful as possible. Because Kim Song-man wrote to many different individuals all over the world, the content of the original letters was often repeated. In order to eliminate repetitious information, and to insure that readers will gain a clear picture of the ordeal and the philosophy of this courageous prisoner of conscience, some of his letters have been edited and/or excerpted with permission.

For the benefit of those who are not familiar with the aims and purposes of Amnesty International, this book also includes descriptions of the progress of the case. Readers may note discrepancies in the spelling of Kim Song-man's name, and the names of the various prisons in which he was incarcerated. We apologize in advance for any confusion this may cause, and for any mistakes in this publication.

Amnesty International's Work

Amnesty International is a worldwide movement of people acting on the conviction that governments must not deny individuals their basic human rights. Recipient of the 1977 Nobel Peace Prize, Amnesty International bases its work on the United Nations Universal Declaration of Human Rights. As part of its campaign to protect fundamental human rights, Amnesty International regularly publishes country reports and other documents on human rights issues around the world. All published information is scrupulously analyzed and cross-checked by our research department and legal offices in London to ensure the integrity of the final reports. These reports are regarded by experts in various fields of study as one of the most reliable sources for information on human rights issues. The accuracy and strict impartiality with which our research is conducted have reinforced our reputation and made us a vital resource for many leading news organizations, government agencies, lawyers, professors, and students. Our publications are invaluable reference tools for any library.

— Amnesty International Catalogue 1995

Amnesty International USA
322 W. 8th Ave
New York, NY 10001
212-807-8400
www.aiusa.org

This link provides information on Amnesty in the USA, including how to get involved and how to make donations.

Prologue

A few pieces of paper started us all on a remarkable journey...

The Amnesty International Case Sheet dated August 1989 provided the "bare bones" description of Kim Song-man's arrest, conviction and sentence. The fact that he was reportedly tortured during interrogation in a   South Korean prison was also noted.

We learned that he was a graduate of Yonsei University, and that he worked in a private language school before he was arrested.

Kim Song-man's "crime" against his country, under the National Security Law, was his peaceful support for the reunification of the two Koreas.

In the Case Sheet document, Amnesty International officials expressed grave concern for the treatment of Kim Song-man. Amnesty International adopted him as a prisoner of conscience and urged the Korean authorities to investigate reports of his torture and mistreatment.

Introduction

Kim Song-man—Posterboy for Amnesty International

Amnesty International created the term "prisoner of conscience" to describe individuals who are imprisoned for their beliefs, or their ethnic origin, sex, color, language, national or social origin, economic status or birth, provided they have not advocated or resorted to violence.

Kim Song-man's case provides a "walking tour" of the Amnesty International mandate. Kim Song-man (KSM for short) was initially held by the South Korean Agency for National Security Planning without access to an attorney. When first taken to jail, he was tortured. Later, he was again denied access to adequate counsel. In fact, KSM argued his own case on appeal up to the Supreme Court of Korea. The case featured what became an infamous "suicide letter" he had been forced to write and sign when first imprisoned. Upon his conviction, KSM was given the death penalty, so he became a Death Penalty case. Later, when KSM's sentence was commuted to life imprisonment, he became a regular Prisoner of Conscience, someone in prison for the non-violent expression of his or her beliefs.

Continuing the "tour" of AI's workings, it is important to note that KSM's file was at first an "Investigation" case, because Amnesty International had not confirmed that his beliefs were non-violent. Once Amnesty International confirmed that KSM had neither used nor advocated violence, his case converted to an "Adoption" case.

Kim Song-man or Seong Man, as he sometimes wrote his name, was moved from prison to prison for over 13 years until President Kim Dae-jung ordered KSM's final unconditional release on 15 August 1998 in celebration of the anniversary of Korea's liberation from Japan.

Over the years, Amnesty Adoption Group #202 (based in Normal, Ill.) wrote letters. But that wasn't all we did. You will see here some of the many activities that go into an Amnesty Group's efforts on behalf of a prisoner. KSM was the subject of a postcard campaign, petition drives, Christmas Card and letter writing campaigns to him and to governmental officials in Korea and abroad. We sent hundreds of "care" packages of books, pens, clothing, food, coffee, chocolate and gum.

With the nearly total coverage of the Amnesty mandate and so many activities, you can understand why we almost called this collection of Kim Song-man's letters "Posterboy".

Amnesty International

SOUTH KOREA
Appeal for the release of Kim Song-man

APRIL 1992

AI INDEX: ASA 25/12/92
DISTR: SC/CO/GR

Amnesty International is calling for the immediate and unconditional release of Kim Song-man who is serving a term of life imprisonment on charges under the National Security Law. Amnesty International believes Kim Song-man is a prisoner of conscience detained for the peaceful exercise of his rights to freedom of expression and association.

Kim Song-man was arrested in June 1985 and accused of conducting espionage activities on behalf of North Korea. He was initially sentenced to death, but this sentence was reduced to life imprisonment under a presidential amnesty in December 1988. Kim Songman is among over 40 political prisoners in Taejon Prison who have refused to sign a statement of "conversion" renouncing their alleged communist beliefs. His family and supporters claim that he has received poor medical treatment during his imprisonment and that he is not normally permitted to receive letters and greetings cards from supporters outside the country. Kim Song-man is a Christian but Amnesty International has been told that he is not permitted to attend Sunday services at the prison. He is reported to suffer from poor concentration as a result of the stress he experienced while under sentence of death. In 1991, a collection of Kim Song-man's letters was published. In one letter he describes the time he spent under sentence of death:

"Never knowing when his sentence will be carried out, a condemned prisoner dies several times a day. Whenever the warden opens the door of his cell, or if the other inmates are not given any exercise in spite of the clear weather, he thinks 'this must be the moment of my death', and his heart jumps. Or if a warden who was formerly cold or cruel to him suddenly changes his demeanour, he thinks of his death. It might be an exaggeration to say several times a day, but certainly once or twice a month, he smells his own death, and he must always be prepared for it.

"Not only the condemned prisoner himself, but his family too undergo the same emotional pain. And if there is an incident in the cell area where the prisoner lives, his family cannot visit him; and every time a prison official puts an unusual stamp on to their visitation paper, the same dreadful thoughts begin again."

Amnesty International has adopted Kim Song-man as a prisoner of conscience as it believes that he is detained solely for his political beliefs and that there is no evidence of his having carried out espionage activities or having used or advocated the use of violence. It is also concerned about reports that he was tortured during his interrogation by the Agency for National Security Planning.

ACTION REQUESTED

Please send appeals to the South Korean Minister of Justice seeking the immediate and unconditional release of Kim Song-man:

Address:
Mr Kim Ki-choon
Minister of Justice
Ministry of Justice
1 Chungang-dong
Kwachon-myon
Shihung-gun
Kyonggi Province
Republic of Korea

The preceding document is a condensed version of the information Group #202 originally received to begin our work. The purpose was to help us understand what we were writing letters about—and to learn more about the human being behind the bars.

Meet Amnesty International Group #202 of Normal, Illinois

Our experiences as an Amnesty Group are typical of most such groups. Our methods are ordinary. Yes, we got discouraged with this case. We took breaks— and then we'd get back at it after awhile. We faced the same hardships of getting around to writing the letters as every other Amnesty group.

Writing short, polite letters is not rocket science. We just required a few nudges to get around to it. We tried to make the experience of being a member of Amnesty a little easier on everyone in the group.

Sharing the Inspiration

The members of Group #202 want this book to inspire people. The letters continue to inspire those of us who initially received them, to appreciate our lives, as KSM seems to enjoy his. We want to bring hope to those who are writing to other prisoners, to write more. That is the purpose of Amnesty International: To inspire hope for a better world. We want to encourage people to join Amnesty International. More deeply, we want this book to inspire people to touch one another, to reach out to communicate, concretely and metaphorically, to write letters. Kim Song-man touched us and we want to share that.

The letters from KSM gave us natural highs that lasted for days, weeks, months. Re-reading the letters revives these highs again and again. We wanted to share those feelings with you, especially with other writers for Amnesty International. We know what thankless work it can seem, writing letters month in and month out on behalf of someone in prison far away, often without hearing anything back. Because Kim Song-man told us specifically and repeatedly, we know what a difference letters make. We wanted to share the feedback we got over the years, so that KSM's letters will continue to inspire others, as they inspire us.

How Amnesty Works

How does Amnesty work? Amnesty members write letters. Each local group's raison d'être is to reach prisoners, and public officials who might influence treatment of a case, with letters. Amnesty members who write on behalf of prisoners feel very fortunate to experience the unique thrill of receiving a letter from "your prisoner." Sometimes letters are simply acknowledged. Other times there is no acknowledgement and no letters of reply from ambassadors or other government officials. In this book you will find examples of feedback from government officials, the prisoner's family, and from the prisoner himself.

Writing Letters for Amnesty Makes a Difference

Amnesty is about making a difference in the world. We got a clear indication that our efforts made a difference. Not all Amnesty members or groups have that positive experience. Yet it is conclusively proven: Amnesty International groups make a clear and definable difference in lives of people who may think about giving up hope. Many times, the AI letters are the only tethers to hope that people have. Yes, YOUR letters have an impact. Collectively, AI makes a gigantic difference to tens of thousands of people every year. Amnesty keeps a candle burning for hope and justice the world over.

We Simplified the Process and Held Meetings by Mail

Group #202 eventually reached a point when attendance at our monthly AI meetings was becoming sparse. The group decided we could communicate much more information more rapidly if we would "Meet by Mail." By doing so, we could all use the time writing letters, which would enable us to generate more letters on behalf of the prisoners.

We held quarterly face-to-face meetings to keep people posted on the latest news. Our goal was to make it easier for everyone to write and to write regularly. We do not know if we sent more letters than other AI groups, or more than we otherwise might have sent, but we did continue to send mail and packages on a regular basis. KSM let us know that the letters and packages arrived, so the plan worked.

Automation made the letter writing easier. Group member Steve Monk would type in the list of Korean officials on a computer and print out a sheet of labels. Every new member or writer would receive a set of pre-addressed labels. When the officials changed, Steve would update and send off another set of labels.

Steve also typed up labels for KSM, every time his address changed. KSM changed prisons about every 6-10 months, so we would make up a new set of labels to send out. Every time KSM was sent to a new prison, we made an effort to send mail and packages directly and quickly, so that the new prison officials would know KSM had someone watching out for his well being. AI Groups from other countries also wrote KSM and received letters, and some of those letters have been included in this book.

An Ordinary Amnesty Group with Extraordinary Good Luck

Aside from the fact we may have a few more retirees than most, we are an ordinary Amnesty group. Group #202 includes a retired minister, a farmer, a housewife, an internal trainer at an insurance company, a retired waitress, an investment broker/money manager, an administrative assistant, a junior high teacher, retired religion and art professors and a retired elementary school teacher.

We all have busy "other lives." We all wrote pretty regularly and shared details of our work, our activities and our families. Our group happened to get lucky by having our prisoner write back. From his letters, it was apparent that KSM appreciated the vicarious view of life in the outside world as much as the items we sent.

Thank you for letting us share our "thrill." May these letters and the stories they represent bring you hope you can spread far and wide the rest of your days. Our Amnesty Group would like to say "Thank you!" to all those who wrote on behalf of Kim Song-man. May your efforts inspire others who work on behalf of a peaceful world.

Drake Zimmerman, Amnesty Adoption Group #202,
Case Coordinator for South Korean Prisoner of Conscience Kim Song-man, a.k.a. Kim Seong Man, 1986 until Case Closed 15 August 1998.
Bloomington-Normal, Illinois
September 2000

Thoughts from Members of AI Group #202

I'm Jerry Stone, Professor Emeritus of Religion at Illinois Wesleyan University in Bloomington, Ill. I wrote Amnesty International letters for more than fifteen years because I wanted to help people who were unjustly imprisoned by despotic, sometimes demonic, political leaders bent on forcing all citizens into conformance with their autocratic governments. Even when the letters didn't bring prisoner release, the simple effort to remember the prisoners through writing letters was important.

The most discouraging experience is to write letters for months, even years, and receive no response. Are the letters getting through? Or maybe they're just dumped. Then suddenly comes a prisoner's response telling you he's received your letter which brought a bright moment in his seemingly endless dark days. Or another time comes the long-awaited news of a prisoner's release!

My advice to letter writers is: write because it's the right thing to do, not just because your efforts will be rewarded. Also, there's a collective energy in the common psychic focus of a large group of people writing letters to accomplish a specific end. A community of people has spoken; their message is out there in the world—there's a kind of mystical power in it! And when prisoner responses and releases do come, your efforts are rewarded more than a hundred-fold.

Jerry H. Stone

It's all about ripples... When I sent my first letter to Kim Song-man, I thought I was simply writing a cheerful note to an obscure, lonely person who might get some comfort from my letters. What happened was quite the opposite. I found him to be an extraordinary person who was resolute in his determination to find meaning and even joy in his circumstances. I began to look forward to his letters and started to share his words of hope with my friends. After a time, people began to ask to see his letters. One co-worker used some of Kim Song-man's thoughts to teach his fifth grade Sunday School class. Just like the ripples in a stream spreading in an ever-widening circle, Kim Song-man's gentle spirit and his message of hope touched people who could not begin to understand his life in a Korean prison cell.

Susan Clary

I am a 74-year-old widow. I retired from Illinois State University in Normal, Ill. in 1990. I started writing for Amnesty over 10 years ago because I wanted to do some good in the world, and writing letters seemed the easiest way.

I wrote some letters and sent some packages to Kim Song-man in Korea. He answered me and I was appalled to learn that the Korean prisons are unheated in winter. I offered, in my ignorance, to send hot water bottles. Kim Song-man thanked me, but said what he really wanted was Wintergreen chewing gum (to be traded).

What impressed me about Kim Song-man was his upbeat spirit, even though confined to a cold cell with one small, high window, through which he could just glimpse one flower in the corner of the prison yard. The only time he saw the trees and flowers was when being transported from one prison to another. In spite of all his long sufferings, he was intending to resume the same work when he was released.

Patricia Madden

Usually when writing to a prisoner of conscience you seldom get a reply and just hope that your letter was received. Kim Song-man was the exception.

I wrote to Kim Song-man to lift his spirits and hopefully to improve his living conditions. After several years, something unexpected began to happen. Kim Song-man started to improve my spirits. He would eloquently write about a flower he saw in the prison yard and I would see a flower the next day and stop to enjoy its radiance, thinking of Song-man. Or he would describe the cold and damp of his prison cell and I would keenly feel and appreciate the comfort and good fortune of my own home.

Over and over in each letter, I would become more cognizant and thankful for all the little good things that made up my life. When small aggravating things would happen to me, I could easily put those things in perspective (by thinking of Song-man) and get through them easily.

I'll always remember Kim Song-man for his sincerity, humor and humbleness. Thank you, Kim Song-man for all you have given and taught me.

Robert A. Connelly

I am a retired minister. I helped found the Amnesty Adoption Group #202 in 1978 with Judy and Jerry Stone and others. I've written letters consistently for over 20 years now. I joined Amnesty after I saw an article about the founders of Amnesty. It was the power of the fine art of friendly persuasion, which is at the heart of my philosophy of life. It is the only way I can stay in the ministry and not be cynical, because I think the spirit of God works in that way.

I have never been in prison myself, but I visited many prisoners because of what Jesus said in the 25th Chapter of Matthew: I was in prison and ye visited me.

(continued on next page)

Prisoners of Conscience can appeal to everybody because of their belief that their nonviolent expression of their philosophy of life can influence the world in which they live. We need these people. And they need us.

What keeps me writing, despite a tremor in my right hand, is my feeling of compassion for people who are suffering for their beliefs. What kept me writing for Kim Song-Man was that I felt a real fellowship with him. I felt that he was a person who was Christian to the core. His letters are filled with the words and the spirit of the Sermon on the Mount. Kim Song-Man's grandfather, I understand, founded the Christian Church in Korea.

My words of advice to other letter writers of Amnesty: Be careful not to send things that will be useless. Ask first before you send things. Prisoners need simple things that have a powerful influence on their capacity to keep on keeping on. Even the most hardened jailers of World War II were affected by sympathy for the undeserved suffering.

N. Grier Hills

Why did I join Amnesty International? In the fall of 1973, I attended language school in Germany. For the last two months I had as a roommate an 18-year-old Greek named Peter. Peter had spent six months in prison as a political prisoner for shooting his mouth off about the generals. Peter told me I wouldn't believe the people who were in prison with him; lawyers, ministers, businessmen and, as he called them, "important people." The government which imprisoned Peter and the others was made infamous in the Costa-Gavras movie, "Z."

When the government changed, they were released. Peter was sent to language school so he could learn German to help in the Greek tourism industry.

One night in October, we all went down to watch the nightly news showing tanks rolling through the streets of Athens. Peter blanched. Visibly shaking, he said, "I can't go back there. Those are the people who put me in prison."

In the next few weeks, he arranged to get asylum in Canada, where he had a brother. I vowed when I got through school and settled that I would do something with Amnesty International.

Ten years later, I was settled and had joined the local Amnesty International Adoption Group #202 in Normal, Ill. Soon after that, Kim Song-man's case came up and I was the case coordinator.

It was as if my friend from school had been grievously wronged and we were at a loss as to how to help him. I knew that but for couple of short twists of fate, I could have been the one who suggested that the two Koreas peacefully reunite and suffered his fate.

So how to help? "Give him hope," came the answer. Write and send packages consistently. Let him know we're here, we'll be here, as long as it takes. Yes, there were moments of hope—and years of uncertainty—writing letters month in and month out. Then word from him! And the letters, as you see, letters we read again and again, passed around and read again. They are like reading blasts of light from extreme darkness. Knowing that not all Amnesty groups or writers are blessed with such gifts, I decided the letters had to be shared.

Through the editing, every person who encountered the letters was more than touched. They were astonished at the light the letters show, and the hope, even in the darkest times—beacons from the spirit that shines within us all. Writing letters kindles that light, that hope. We recognize that "lighting a candle" allows us to find each other, to find ourselves, and to navigate the darkness. May these letters brighten your spirit as they have brightened ours. Thank you for writing.

Keep going!

Drake Zimmerman

Part One

Case Information

The Western Illinois Spy Ring Case?

Spies in Macomb, Illinois? When we first heard of Kim Song-man's (KSM) case, we thought the title was something of a joke. Spying on what, corn and soybeans? Western Illinois University is not known as a hotbed of radicalism. One member of our Adoption Group is a farmer. He commented that somebody might have found a radical or two in the Ag Department at University of Illinois, but five radicals at Western Illinois University was unlikely. We still get a chuckle out of the case name.

The Amnesty Group at WIU started writing on behalf of KSM and the others as soon as they heard they had been imprisoned. The local group notified Amnesty International (AI) of the situation. AI wanted to gather all the facts before they made KSM and the others an official "Adoption Case." An Adoption Case is a long-term commitment by an AI group to write letters on behalf of a particular prisoner. For the first several months, the KSM case was simply an "investigation case", until AI verified the facts.

Members of the AI group in Macomb who had known KSM were so certain of his non-violent views that they began writing letters on his behalf right away. Once the case was formally adopted by AI in 1986, the scope of support was broadened and AI asked Group #202 in Normal, Ill. to take on the case.

What follows is an excerpt from an AI case overview issued in 1989.

You may want to come back to pages 25 - 28. We include this much-edited description of the case to show that AI gives Adoption Groups outstanding detailed background and guidance through the process of letter writing. Case information sheets provide addresses, suggestions on what to say—and what NOT to say—and much more. AI follows up with constant, timely updates on the changes in cases and politics of the country involved.

Amnesty's involvement in tens, nay, hundreds of thousands of cases around the globe has honed their skills of diplomacy to a high art form. Politness varies by culture, as does what works—and what doesn't.

Excerpted from AI External Document
Reference/ AI Index: ASA 25/24/89 Distr: SC/CO/GR

September 1989

SOUTH KOREA

THE 1985 "WESTERN ILLINOIS UNIVERSITY SPY RING" CASE

In September 1985 the South Korean military and civilian security agencies jointly announced the arrest of 20 people, mostly students, on charges of being North Korean agents and instigating campus unrest under North Korean instructions. The three main defendants, Yang Dong-hwa, Kim Song-man and Hwang Tae-kwon, had
studied at Western Illinois University in Macomb, Illinois, United
States of America in 1982-1983, where they met, and had later moved
to New York. During their stay in the USA they are said to have read
widely about political science and the political system in North
Korea. When announcing the arrests, the security authorities reported the three had attended some events on the Western Illinois
University campus such as the showing of a film on the Kwangju
insurrection of May 1980 and a public talk by a visiting Quaker
leader, Hahm Sok-hon. They accused them of having been influenced
by the publisher of a Korean language paper in New York whom the
South Korean authorities described as a North Korean "collaborator."
The paper Haeuiminbo (Overseas Korean News) reportedly gave
wide coverage to human rights violations and dissidents' activities in
South Korea and called for the withdrawal of US troops from South
Korea and the reunification of the Korean peninsula. The publisher,
a Korean who holds US nationality, allegedly showed the three stu-
dents video films of North Korea and arranged meetings with Yang
Dong-hwa and Kim Song-man and North Korean officials, in
Hungary and East Berlin, in the case of Kim Song-man, and in
Pyongyang itself, the capital of North Korea, in the case of Yang
Dong-hwa. During these meetings, the South Korean authorities said
they received political indoctrination and instructions to engage in
anti-government activities and passed information to the North
Koreans on the student movement in the south. Hwang Tae-kwon is
alleged to have received "espionage" training directly from the publisher in New York. After their return to South Korea, separately in

1983 and 1984, Yang Dong-hwa and Kim Song-man renewed contact with activist students, some of whom were also arrested in this case. Both are said to have set up small study circles and to have supplied North Korean literature to students. Kim Song-man also wrote theoretical articles on the political situation. Hwang Tae-kwon was arrested at Kimpo airport as he was returning from a vacation in June 1985.

All the arrests are believed to have taken place in June or July 1985, after the arrest of many student leaders in May. The prisoners were held incommunicado during their interrogation by the Agency for National Security Planning (ANSP) until 5 August and were reportedly tortured.

Their trial started in October 1985. Yang Dong-hwa, Kim Song-man and Hwang Tae-kwon were accused of being the "ring leaders" of "anti-state" organizations (that is student groups) and of having engaged in subversive activities under instructions from North Korea. The others were accused of having been recruited by the "ringleaders" and of carrying out various anti-government activities under their orders, such as listening to North Korean broadcasts, organizing violent demonstrations, taking part in study groups and giving to the "ringleaders" pamphlets and documents on the student movement, which the latter allegedly subsequently gave to North Korean officials or agents abroad. The importance of the case lay primarily in the fact that two of the main defendants had had illegal contacts with North Korean officials and the third with an alleged pro-North Korean agent, but also in that they had provided a new theoretical foundation for the student movement. This emphasized the role of the USA in Korean politics and other views that are also held by the government of North Korea.

The first trial was before the Seoul District Criminal Court with courtroom access limited mostly to family members and lawyers. According to several sources, the prisoners' families were intimidated into not engaging human rights lawyers for the first trial and the prisoners were represented by state-appointed lawyers. Observers at one of the hearings noted that the students spoke in their own defense in the absence of the state-appointed lawyers. On 20 January 1986, the court sentenced Yang Dong-hwa and Kim Song-man to death. Hwang Tae-kwon and Kang Yong-ju, a student leader from Kwangju, were given sentences of life imprisonment; nine others were sentenced to terms ranging from two to ten years and four were released with suspended sentences. The sentences were upheld by the Seoul High Court on 31 May 1986 and by the Supreme Court on 3 December 1986. Most of the prisoners had their sentences reduced under a presidential amnesty in December 1988: the death sentences were reduced to life imprisonment, the life sentences to 20 years' imprisonment. Six prisoners remain in detention in this case.

From 1986 to 1988, Amnesty International campaigned for the commutation of the death sentences on Yang Dong-hwa and Kim Song-man. It made inquiries about the prisoners with the authorities and other sources of information. In the case of Kim Song-man and Hwang Tae-kwon, Amnesty International has now been able to collect enough information to show that they are prisoners of conscience, detained for their peaceful political activities and opinions and that they did not engage in "espionage." In the case of the other prisoners, further inquiries about the charges and evidence against them as well as about their political activities prior to their arrests are required.

Kim Song-man was born in 1957 and graduated in physics from Yonsei University in Seoul in February 1981. He comes from a Christian family and his grandfather founded the Evangelical Church in Korea. In his student days he was involved in political activities and was a member of the Christian Student Association. He went to the USA in June 1982 and enrolled at Western Illinois University to study political science. The following year he moved to New York and, according to some reports, contributed articles to Haeuiminbo (Overseas Korean News). In June 1983 he visited Europe and stayed at the North Korean embassy in Budapest, Hungary, for three days and discussed the student movement and the political situation in South Korea. He received $5000 as travel expenses from the embassy staff.

According to the indictment, Kim Song-man was encouraged by the North Koreans he met to engage in anti-government activities and was given instructions such as to encourage student activists to enter the Korean Military Academy. Kim Song-man has denied receiving any instructions or carrying them out; the only evidence to support the accusation is his confession, which he claims he made under torture. He has said that he met North Koreans to learn more about North Korea and to find out about the possibilities for Korean reunification.

Kim Song-man returned to South Korea in July 1983 and worked in the language laboratory of a private foreign language institute. He again became involved in the student movement and, according to the authorities, formed a group called Chonminjunghoe (The Entire People Association) in the Seoul area. In May 1984 he wrote a pamphlet entitled "Subordination and Battle Cry." The pamphlet described the USA as "imperialists" and anti-communism as a "Cold War theory to prolong the territorial division [of Korea]" and, the authorities say, was widely quoted by anti-government student publications. Kim Song-man is also accused of having hung a wall poster in Tongguk University in Seoul, which claimed the presence of (US) nuclear weapons in South Korea could lead to a world crisis, and of having distributed leaflets supporting the occupation of the US Information Centre in Seoul by students in May 1985.

Kim Song-man had, it seemed, remained in contact with the publisher of Haeuiminbo in New York, who apparently facilitated his visit to East Germany in November 1984. On this occasion Kim spent three or four days in East Berlin and gave to the North Korean embassy staff copies of his pamphlet "Subordination and Battle Cry" and of another leaflet entitled "Criticism of Night School—A study on the political conscientization of workers." This gave rise to the charges in the indictment that he had passed national secrets to North Korea. Again the discussion seems to have focussed on the general trends of the South Korean student movement. Kim was reportedly invited to join the Workers' Party but refused and, according to him, expressed strong criticisms of the North Korea "juche" (self-reliance) philosophy. Again he was reportedly given and accepted $10,000 as travel expenses. He also arranged to receive North Korean publications, material which was banned in South Korea.

Kim Song-man was arrested on 6 June 1985. In an appeal to the Supreme Court on 14 August 1986, he wrote:

> "I am a person who wishes the independence of our nation and democracy. I think that this ideal can be realized in a socialistic country. I was interrogated and tortured mercilessly at the Agency for National Security Planning. During the interrogation and torture I was even forced to write a suicide letter addressed to my parents in order to disguise my possible death as a suicide. The press widely published my forced confession as though it was true. I only long for the day we can enjoy our independence from under slavish submission to a foreign power. Even if all the world does not believe me I know that God knows the truth."

Kim Song-man was sentenced to death by the courts. His sentence was commuted to life imprisonment under the December 1988 presidential amnesty. He is currently held in Seoul prison.

Amnesty International has adopted Kim Song-man as a prisoner of conscience as it believes that there is no evidence of his having carried out espionage activities or having used or advocated the use of violence. It is calling for his immediate and unconditional release.

KSM had his annual visit outside the prison and was able to share his Wrigley's gum. He writes about desiring "a life of rendering aid" to others and sharing joy with them.

"Execution of a death sentence will happen at any time except holidays. I didn't know when I would be hanged. It could be tomorrow, the day after tomorrow or today. It gave me bitter grief to be separated from my dear family and the world and to leave my work in my youth. I lived in deep sorrow in the long period."

—Kim Song-man in a letter to David W. Babson,
6/14/96

Part Two

What We Did to Help Kim Song-man
Post cards, petitions and presents

In the first years, Kim Song-man was not allowed to write letters to foreigners. We did send letters and received responses from his mother, Choi In-hwa, and some government officials. We also conducted post card and petition campaigns. Amnesty International organized the production of a short music video feature on KSM as well. The video ("Pour Kim Song-man) was directed by noted director Constantin Costa-Gavras and produced in French for a French audience.

In several of her letters, Choi In-hwa referred to a book of letters and essays KSM wrote during this time. The material was published by the human rights group Minkahyup to help free political prisoners. She sent us some copies. We did not get the book translated, but we did use the illustrations you see throughout this book.

The Post Card Campaign

Our efforts to help Kim Song-Man included included several special campaigns. Our first campaign featured post cards. We printed up 10,000 postcards with a picture of KSM. We addressed them to the Korean Ambassador to the US and included a message. Distribution for several hundred of the cards was handled by the AI Monthly Mailing. We included a post card and a place to call for more cards. Over the course of three to four months, groups from all over the US and Canada called and sent us letters about participating in our Post Card Campaign.

The Petition Campaign

Sometime in early 1987, we decided to make up a petition calling for the review of KSM's case and his release, and advocating the release of the other prisoners of the Western Illinois Spy Ring Case. AI's monthly mailing distributed the petition and encouraged other groups to make copies and get as many signatures as possible.

Sending mail to Korea involves costly overseas postage, so we promised to send copies of the petitions to the Korean Government onbehalf of the groups, if they would send us a copy of the petitions.

We ended up with a foot high stack of petitions! We sent one complete set of copies to the Ambassador and one set to the then new President of the Republic of Korea. The Attaché at the Korean Embassy in Chicago declined a meeting, so we only sent off the two copies.

Before sending the petitions to the Korean President and Ambassador, we faxed copies to the Korean Embassy. We faxed almost every night and weekend for months. It was probably a nuisance to them to receive strings of petitions almost nightly for a while. We do not know what impact the cards and petitions had on the recipients, or on the treatment of KSM, but because we sent such a great quantity of mail, it would have been difficult to ignore the message.

When Kim Young-sam became president of the Republic of Korea, we sent him a copy of the petitions, and made a copy for the new Ambassador.

Quantity is Quality — The Quantity Campaign

We decided to write KSM directly, to see if that would have any impact. Our group also sent him items on a fairly regular basis to keep the prison officials on notice that someone was paying attention to his case.

What to send? Once he was allowed to write to us, we learned from some of his first letters that there was no heat in Korean prisons. Winter was coming. We decided on scarves, gloves, hand warmers, sweaters, sweatshirts, socks and other practical items. What KSM could not use he could trade to other prisoners.

To make sending packages easier, we got labels from the post office and sent them to all our members, with details on how much postage would be needed. We had to take our packages to the post office to be weighed, but otherwise, they were ready to go.

In my office, I usually made up a dozen or so packages at a time. I could then space them out to arrive over a period of time. I knew the packages might arrive at the same time at the prison in Korea, roughly six weeks later, because they were on the same boat, but that did not matter. My goal was to have regular contact with KSM. When I had not sent packages for a while, I would typically send the first couple weeks' packages by airmail, and then followed up with more packages by boat mail.

The Cocoa Campaign

We kept asking KSM what we could send—what he wanted and what would be of use. We had sent him Ivory Soap, socks and other items as a result. We discovered that, at certain times of the year, KSM had access to a stove and could make coffee and cocoa. So we went down to a local store and got small jars of coffee and packets of instant cocoa. A few packets would fit in a mailing envelope. The hot chocolate (hot C mix) packets were always gratefully acknowledged and enjoyed by KSM until his final prison stay in 1998. KSM wrote that the officials at that prison were not sure what the powder in the instant chocolate contained, and would not allow him to accept it, so we could not send any more.

Should Another Group Take Over the KSM Case?

About 1993, more than five years into the case, our group decided that we were not sending many letters or packages and that the case deserved the extra energy that another group might give it. We contacted Michael O'Reilly, the AI Coordinator of cases. When we told him how many (we thought, how "few") letters and packages we were sending, Michael gently told us we were nuts, that we were doing a wonderful job and to hang in there!

Breakthrough: The First Letter Abroad

After receiving reassurances from Michael O'Reilly, we resumed our letter writing and continued to send packages, even though, as an "unconverted" prisoner, Kim Song-man was not allowed to reply to us. We took our inspiration from an AI publication quoting a prisoner who claimed to have received better treatment after receiving hundreds of letters.

"I remember your friends who sent me letters and parcels. I could receive them but to my regret I couldn't reply. Please give my best regards to them and tell them that I really wanted to say 'thank you.'"

—Kim Song-man in a letter to Drake Zimmerman

October 8, 1993

"When the first 200 letters came, the guards gave me back my clothes. Then the next 200 came, and the prison director came to see me. When the next pile of letters arrived, the director got in touch with his superior. The letters kept coming and coming: three thousand of them. The president was informed. The letters still kept arriving, and the president called the prison and told them to let me go.

"After I was released, the president called me to his office. He said: 'How is it that a trade union leader like you has so many friends from all over the world?' He showed me an enormous box full of letters he had received and, when we parted, he gave them to me."

— *Julio de Pena Valdez, released prisoner of conscience from the Dominican Republic*

—Amnesty International

A Warden's Heart Was Touched By the Packages

By this time, most of the packages we sent got through. We knew the Quantity Campaign really worked when KSM wrote that he was given permission to write us letters because the prison warden had seen the quantity of packages arriving week after week, month after month. The warden did not know who KSM was, but was so moved by the quantity and consistency of packages that KSM got better treatment. KSM's letters always indicated that our gifts were a comfort to him. We would like to think that what we did made a difference to his life. You can judge for yourself.

In any case, it worked. The first letter from KSM arrived in October of 1993. He had written it on my birthday, which made it an extra special treat. Here it is:

8 Oct 93

Dear Drake Zimmerman,

Now I am very happy to write a letter to you. I have received a large number of parcels and have been eager to write you letters. In Korea a political prisoner is normally forbidden to send letters to a man in a foreign country except his family or his near relative. But in August I met and talked with the chief of the department of correctional affairs in the prison and obtained permission to send you letters. What moved him to change his mind and grant me the permission was the quantity of parcels which have been sent me by you for about two years. The great number of parcels didn't mean anything but your warm heart and extraordinary human sincerity. They moved him. It has been more than eight years since I wrote a letter to a foreigner. This is the first time for me to write an overseas letter in the prison. Drake Zimmerman, thank you from the bottom of my heart.

My daily life is monotonous and changeless. An hour is given per day I have to stay in the small single room. Everything in my life is all the same everyday. But there is one thing which changes clearly everyday in my routine life. It is the contents of books which I read everyday. Nowadays I read books on human relations and leadership.

The economic books which you sent me were very helpful. Thank you very much.

I remember your friends who sent me letters and parcels. I could receive them but to my regret I couldn't reply. Please give my best regards to them and tell them that I really wanted to say "thank you."

What I consider as the most important thing is a life of social value. As long as I pursue a life of social value, I can feel the peace of mind and freedom. The conviction that my life is of social value and the vision of future society will come true makes me endure the present pain much easier.

While I was writing this letter, I received the birthday card you sent me. Thank you very much. The written expression of health, comfort, growth, and great ideas is very satisfactory to me. I hope the coming year will bring you them, too. I will be 37 on Oct. 10. And I was notified that some parcels sent to me from U.S.A. had arrived at the prison. I didn't receive them yet. I guess you sent them. Thank you again for your kindness.

Sincerely yours,
Kim Seong Man

GROUP CORRESPONDENCE

In a Group Correspondence letter dated January 12, 1994, Clare McVey of AI's Korea Reseach Team passed along news of Kim Song-man. She noted that the human rights group Minkahyop received word that KSM was held in solitary confinement at Andong Prison—he was the only prisoner in the cellblock—completely isolated. He wrote to his family that "...the only sounds he hears are the ones he makes himself."

Clare noted that his family was worried about KSM, in spite of the otherwise cheerful tone of his letter. She urged us to write lots of cards and letters, even though it was uncertain if the authorities in the prison would allow him to receive the correspondence. For that reason, she also suggested we write to KSM's family or to the Minkahyup group to let them know what we sent to him.

In addition, this letter to AI Groups in France, Belgium, Sweden, and our group in Normal, Illinois, indicated it might be useful for us to express our concern for Kim Song-man's welfare and his status as an AI Prisoner of Conscience.

A fellow Rotarian, Nancy Froelich, served on the Board of Regents for Western Illinois University. When I spoke about Amnesty at her Rotary club, she was so moved by the story of KSM, she bought a T-shirt, which I sent to him. The fairly immediate feedback from KSM thrilled us all.

January 15, 1994

Dear Drake Zimmerman,

I am very pleased to write a letter to you. I received three post-cards you had sent me to Andong prison where I am now. I have also received two books—Webster's New World Dictionary and the 7 Habits of Highly Effective people. I have made a study of personali-ty, human relations and leadership for more than half a year and the book the 7 Habits of Highly Effective people will be very helpful to me. I really want to thank you for your kindness to choose and send me the book which is adequate to my study. The dictionary will be very useful to me too.

Half a month ago I received a package transferred from Kwangju prison. There was a T-shirt inside. The mark of Western Illinois University was printed on it. Can you imagine how I was amazed to receive it? It carried my thought to the past happy WIU days and reminded me of the beautiful scenery of WIU campus. I am anxious to see the campus again. I attached the T-shirt on the wall for deco-ration. It was too precious to me to wear out.

Andong prison is farther than Kwangju prison from Seoul where my parents live. It takes four hours and half by bus from Seoul. The long distance makes my mother exhausted whenever she comes here. She is 67 years old.

I live on the first floor of a three storied building. No other prison-ers live with me. There are only two men —I and a prison guard on the first floor. I have a meal, take exercise ... only by myself. I can never meet prisoners who live on other floors or in other buildings. In general prisoners live a collective life. But I am isolated and under close surveillance. I think it's because I am a well-known political prisoner. Reading books and searching for truth I surmount my lone-liness and yearning for people.

Would you please send me a photograph of you and your family? I wish I could see your features.

I always feel grateful for your warm kindness.

Yours sincerely,
Kim Seong Man

Around the end of 1993, we hit upon the idea to have Western Illinois University invite Kim Song-man back to complete his studies. This would give the government the opportunity to get KSM out of the country and to have an excuse, a pretext to set him free. We contacted the University and Charles Weston, chair of the Political Science Department, issued an invitation for KSM to apply for readmission to WIU. The plan didn't work, but it did gain publicity for our efforts.

Ambassador Han Seung-Soo
Embassy of Republic of Korea
2450 Mass Ave. NW
Washington, DC 20008   18 February 1994

Your Excellency: Re: Kim Seong-Man's Release to Study at
                            Western Illinois Univ. 1994

There is one matter I would like to help you resolve. Kim Seong-Man is now being held in Andong Prison, #1310. He has served 8 years in prison. I am certain you are aware of the details of his case. It may be time to consider granting his release.

Perhaps I can help. It has come to my attention that Kim Seong-Man has received an invitation to resume his graduate studies at Western Illinois University. I volunteer to pay his passage to Illinois in the United States and to underwrite his education there for the period of time needed to finish his Master's degree. Would you please consider releasing him to resume his studies and to begin a productive life? You now have the ability to solve the problem of Kim Seong-Man quickly and smoothly.

Would you be so kind as to review the situations of Kim Seong-Man and those similarly situated? For Kim Seong-Man, you now have a means to remedy his situation. If you allow him to resume his studies at Western Illinois University. I would be happy to help you solve similar situations.

Thank you so much for your efforts to improve the human rights situation in your country and for your efforts in the future.

Yours,   *Drake Zimmerman*

Drake Zimmerman JD CFA Zimmerman & Armstrong Investment Advisors, Inc.
Paul Harris Fellow and Past President, Rotary Club of Normal, Illinois
encl: Invitation to Resume Studies, Western III U.
cc: Senator Paul Simon, Washington, DC USA
        U.S. Department of State, Korea Desk
        President Kim Young Sam
        Fred Kardon, Executive Managing Editor, The Daily Pantagraph,
            as part of article on Kim Seong-Man for syndication

Consul General John Ratigan   via FAX 0 11-82-2-73 8-8845
U.S. Embassy
Chongru-ku
Seoul, Republic of Korea   23 February 1994

Dear Sir: re: Kim Seong-Man's Visa to Return to Western
               Illinois University

For several years I have been working on behalf of a South Korean "Prisoner of Conscience" named Kim Seong-Man. He was part of the "Western Illinois Spy Ring Case," with which you may be familiar. Kim Seong-Man is now being held in solitary confinement in Andong Prison, #1310. He has served 8 years in prison. I am certain you are aware of the details of his case. I am a member of Amnesty International. I am also a Rotarian, Past President of the Normal, Illinois club and work at times to solve particular problems in the world. We may now have an opportunity to achieve KSM's release.

Kim Seong-Man has received an invitation to resume his graduate studies at Western Illinois University. I personally volunteer to pay his passage to Western Illinois University in the United States and to underwrite his education there for the period of time needed to finish his Master's degree. I'd even come get him, if need be.

Would you be able to help him obtain a Visa to study in the US? There is no assurance that they will let him out of prison to study, but it is worth a try. (If you have any other suggestions, please contact me.) What we want is a document, a piece of paper to show the Republic of Korean government that would be prima facie evidence that Kim Seong-Man is (or could be) eligible for a Visa, if released. If you need to interview him, he is in prison at Andong. Technically, I am not sure whether you are able to make a prejudgment as to his eligibility for a Visa.

What the Koreans require for a student to study abroad is not known. Any help you may offer is greatly appreciated.

I have spoken with the Korean Desk at the State Department, Lynn Turk knows the case well. Senator Paul Simon's office is writing (more) letters on his behalf would be happy to help: Drew Orufer (202) 224-2152 FAX (202) 224-0868. 462 Dirksen Office Building, Washington, DC 20510-1302 has helped us over the years. I have a stack of petitions literally over a foot high on behalf of KSM.

Thank you so much for your efforts to improve the human rights situation in your country and for your efforts in the future. Any help you can provide would be greatly appreciated.

Yours,   *Drake Zimmerman*

Drake Zimmerman JD CFA Zimmerman & Armstrong Investment Advisors, Inc.
Paul Harris Fellow and Past President, Rotary Club of Normal, Illinois

I sent a book on meditation to KSM, thinking meditation might help him relieve stress and endure solitude. The book sparked him to write about the stress he had experienced. I don't know how this (or many other letters) got past the censors. In his letter, KSM mentions the state of mind he cultivated in the face of death, even as his friends died. At the end, he asks us to send him chocolate and candy, which we did.

3/18/94

Dear Drake Zimmerman,

I was very delighted to receive the pictures. You look very smart and younger than I imagined. The smile of you and your sister is felt to be bright and attractive. Your wife seems to be intellectual and mild. Thank you for sending me the pictures. I feel sorry not to be able to send you my picture taken in the prison.

As for foreign languages, I can make myself understood in Japanese and English. It is more convenient for me to speak, read and write Japanese than English even though I spent much more time learning English than Japanese. I think it's because word order of the Japanese language is similar to that of the Korean language. 9 years inexperience has brought me weak ability in English, especially in speaking and listening ability. I have hardly spoken English and listened to someone speak English for 9 years, and it was for the first time that I wrote English sending you a letter. But I think 6 months training after release will bring me the former ability in English. I wonder which foreign language is the most useful besides English and Japanese. Which language do you think is the most useful in leading a life internationally and making friends?

Thank you for sending me "Meditation Workbook." It will be helpful. Many prisoners are thought to meditate to overcome stress in the way which is very similar to the way indicated in the book. May I mention the stress which I overcame when I was a prisoner under sentence of death? There were about ten political prisoners who were under sentence of death in the Seoul Detention Institution. Almost all of them changed their minds and tried to give aid to the dictatorial government. They strove to be granted a commutation to life imprisonment desperately. I wished to be granted a commutation, too.

But I couldn't help the dictatorial government. It was out of the bounds of possibility that I would be a helper to the dictatorship. Some people have a feeling that all is vanity in life. They think that life is itself vain and groundless. In a sense I agree with them. But I have the belief that we can surmount the frailty of life making our lives creative and socially valuable. It would deprive me of the meaning of life to be a helper to the dictatorial government. I would have no choice but to be faced with the frailty of life even if I could be granted a commutation as a result of falling away. The sense of meaninglessness of my life would bring mental pain and entire exhaustion.

Being under sentence of death, I preferred death to a life against the people. The only way to be left to me was to walk to the execution ground in a calm manner and with facial expression in peace. Nobody knows when execution is performed. The date could be tomorrow, the day after tomorrow or this afternoon. I should never fail be ready for death even one moment. It was only the peace of mind that would ensure a tranquil attitude on the date of execution. Cultivating my mind, I tried not to lose the peace of mind day after day for two years and three months after an irrevocable judgement of death sentence. In consequence of cultivation of my mind I have often heard that my facial expression looked the most tranquil in the prison.

Political prisoners around me are said to be much impressed by my facial expression and peaceful life. Now four of them have become members of the National Assembly and sometimes come to the prison to meet me. Those who made desperate efforts to be granted a commutation and gave aid to the dictatorial government felt strong stress from the sentence of death and became fretful and nervous. Ironically most of them died, but I was saved.

Foreign institutions of human rights such as Amnesty International and foreign and domestic individuals that tried to save my life do I thank from the bottom of my heart and can I never thank enough.

All packages sent to me are opened in the presence of me. The prison officer who takes charge of postal matter carries packages to me and opens them himself. He picks out some items which prisoners can't possess. Drugs such as aspirin and anodyne, and a digestive are not permitted. The others are handed over to me on the spot. If a package contains a letter, I can read it without fail. (It usually takes more than one month to get the packages in my room after you send them in U.S.A.) Most of the items you have chosen are useful to me. I love lotion, toothpaste, and soap especially. As for tissue and razors, we are provided with them in plenty by the authorities. May I suggest an idea? If some packages contain something to eat in a small quantity such as chocolate, candy and so on, I will eat with the prison officer who delivers packages to me and we can, I think, form closer friendship eating together.

Yours sincerely,
Kim Seong Man

In this letter KSM writes about the sense of duty he feels to his parents and how it pains him to be unable to fulfill that duty. He is starting to connect the members of AI Group #202 who write to him. The comments and mention of writing a letter to the Belgian AI Case Coordinator, Malcolm Purves, encouraged us that the AI process was working. Quantity is quality!

4 May 1994

Dear Drake Zimmerman,

Thank you for the letter and the materials for the Malaria Project. I was astonished to know that Malaria still killed so many people every year. Moreover it makes our heart hurt that most of the victims are children. How mournful are their parents! The Malaria Project is thought to be full of meaning. I hope the Project will end in successful accomplishment.

I appreciate your kind consideration to let me know who David W. Babson and Steven Monk were. It was not until I received your letter that I knew their profession and detailed connection with you. I received postcards from them repeatedly. I am deeply grateful to them. The pictures on the postcards they have sent me were all interesting. Who is Julie Boswell? I have often received letters from Julie Boswell.

Two packages arrived at the prison last month. One was lotion from you and the other was tissue, the legal pad, etc., from Bob Connelly. Fragrant lotion makes me feel happy as I am in unsanitary environment giving out bad smell. Sweet-smelling lotion is too precious to me. Thank you for sending me lotions. (Lotion sent by package post is generally not handed over to prisoners except such lotion in a small case as you sent me.) What Bob Connelly sent was very helpful, too. And I was very pleased to find peanuts in the package. We, I and the prison guard, had a good time eating it—that I can't get or purchase in the prison. I received and read the letter enclosed in the package. Would you please send him my gratitude for the package and the letter? I feel as if I actually see a good-natured man surrounded with lovable children.

I feel at ease though I have lived in the prison for a long time. It's because I have my forties, fifties, and sixties to live an active life in the society. They are long period enough to realize the meaning of my life. I think it makes one happy to make preparations for the future. I feel in peace when I study or cultivate my mind. But there is one thing that makes me sad and unhappy. It is that I can't practice filial piety to my parents. According to Korean custom parents find themselves worth living sacrificing themselves for their children and the children find pleasures of life serving their parents with devotion. Filial devotion is the best virtue in Korea. My parents are getting older. My father is 72 years old and my mother is 68 years old. At present it is the most sorrowful that I can't live with my parents and practice filial duty to them.

Yours sincerely,
Kim Seong-Man

P.s. You were the first foreigner whom I was given leave to communicate with by letters. The permission was extremely difficult to obtain. But after it became less difficult to obtain permission to send letters to foreign countries. I inform you that I sent a letter to Malcolm Purves in Belgium a few days ago

NOTE: The Malaria Project referred to in the preceding letter is a special campaign undertaken by the Normal Rotary Club and other chapters of Rotary International around the world. Through the efforts of Rotarians, education, funds for microscopes, medicines and preventive measures have helped reduce the spread of Malaria and the number of deaths from the disease in such places as the country of Malawi (Pop. 10,000,416) in southern Africa. As a member of the Normal Rotary Club, I have been an active proponent of this project.

Here KSM mentions being moved from prison to prison. Sometimes his English misses a nuance; he calls Mr. Yang in the next cell his "accomplice." We might call him a "fellow accused," not admitting guilt. Note also his reference to the extreme heat in his cell.

7/6/94

Dear Drake Zimmerman,

I was moved from Andong prison to Taegu prison on 6/27/94. Taegu prison is 2 hours distance by car from Andong prison. But it is almost same distance from Seoul, the capital where my parents live.

Taegu prison was built so many years ago that the buildings have been worn out. The toilet in my room is not a flush toilet. But I am not lonely as I was in Andong prison. My accomplice, Mr. Yang, lives in the next room but one, and there are many other prisoners on the same floor. I feel as if I came back to mundane life from a quiet Buddhist temple in a mountain.

Meditation is helpful to my health. I meditate every day. I think it is very useful in keeping my body and mind spirited.

Is Malaria Project going well? Did you get friendly support from the people whom you met in Washington, D.C.? There is a Korean proverb which says, "One's life is heavier than the world." I hope that by virtue of Malaria Project many people will be saved and live lives which are the grace of God.

It is very hot here. It is higher than 35 degrees C in my room in these days. Sultry heat keeps on far into the night. Writing this letter, I am dripping with sweat.

Yours sincerely,
Kim Seong-Man

The watercolor paints I sent were an obvious hit with KSM and the prisoner next door. The German grammar was easy—I have two degrees in German. I sent KSM a whole row of small German books in the months that followed. Per Lindberg of the Swedish AI Group writing for KSM obtained a Korean-German dictionary for him. (See the letter confirming this gift on page 48.)

8/15/94

Dear Drake Zimmerman,

I received packages including watercolor with thanks. Watercolor is useful to me. A political prisoner who lives in next room but one to me is in these days lost in drawing pictures. He was beside himself to see the watercolor. I will use it together with him. I am grateful to you for sending me packages.

I received a postcard and letters, too. I pay my tribute to you for your passion for the Malaria Project. I feel joyful and happy whenever I think lots of lives will be saved from death owing to the Malaria Project. Recently the political prisoner who was delighted to see the watercolor said to me, "Nowadays hell is emptied. There are said to be no devils in hell." I asked why. He said, "Because all the devils have gone to Rwanda." I think that at least one of angels is absent from Heaven, too. I think he is on earth saving lives of people who are dying of malaria.

I am absorbed in studying German in these days. The experience to have learned English is of great help, and German is not felt to be very difficult. But it is regrettable that in my country I can't get a dictionary of German Grammar. I remember that when I learned English, a dictionary of English grammar was greatly helpful to improvement in my knowledge of English. Would you please get a dictionary of German grammar or a book which gives full details of German grammar like a dictionary? I want the book to be written in English.

Sultriness is said to continue till the end of August in this summer. But it is a little cool today, for a typhoon is approaching to Korea.

I am always grateful to you. Please give my best regards to Steven F. Monk.

Yours sincerely,
Kim Seong-Man

GROUP CORRESPONDENCE

Amnesty International Korea Research Team member Sylvia Lindsay shared more news in a Group Correspondence letter dated November 9, 1994. Clare McVey and AI Secretary General Pierre Sane visited South Korea and met with KSM's mother, Choi In-hwa. At the time, she was ailing and suffered from high blood pressure, and she was very worried about her son's health, according to their report.

"...He gets very nervous and finds it hard to sleep, his blood pressure is high and he has digestive problems," noted Sylvia. The letter went on to say that Choi In-Hwa attributed her son's ill-health to the stress of living under a sentence of death for an extended period of time. The good news in this letter was that Taegu Prison afforded KSM a little more contact with other prisoners during recreation periods, and a fellow prisoner who had some knowledge of traditional medicine was able to advise him about foods to avoid to improve his condition.

Sylvia's letter also conveyed Choi In-Hwa's concern that her son received "poorer treatment than others" because of his steadfast refusal to "convert. " She said the prison authorities continued to pressure KSM, but that he considered "conversion" to be an admission of guilt.

Even with the prospect that the authorities might change the title of the "conversion statement" to give it a "softer message," Choi In-hwa said her son would not agree to "convert."

11/5/94

Dear Drake Zimmerman,

I have received books sent by you several times and a birthday card, too. I feel deep gratitude for your constant kindness and warm concern. I am really sorry not to have sent you a birthday card. I hope you forgive me.

I have read with deep concern the articles in the Pantagraph which were enclosed with the birthday card. I am very delightful to know that your will to eliminate malaria and save lives has been recognized over the world. I am proud of you. When I read in the Pantagraph the sentence "Over the course of the next decade, we'll probably save more than a million lives." I in my heart paid respect to you who made an important contribution to human life.

I am in good health. I was moved to a new room in another building a week ago. The prior room was on the upper floor of a two-storied building and commanded a fine view. I could see beautiful mountains and a village outside the prison. But the new room is on the first floor of a two-storied building. Now I can see only the opposite building and the walls of the prison. On the other hand other conditions are much better than before. It is still and I can read books without hindrance of noises and the toilet is flush one. The prior toilet was a conventional type. I am pleased not to smell a bad smell. What makes me most pleased is that I can play on a new playground which has a small tennis court. I can play tennis for an hour everyday. I think it will be helpful not only to my physical health but also to my mental health. I am no more than a beginner. Now I am learning tennis very hard.

I have received a birthday card from Julie, too. Her handwriting is a little hard to read, and it makes me very interested in reading her letter. I love her handwriting. By the way, I don't know who she is. Will you please let me know who she is?

Yours sincerely,
Kim Seong Man

P.s. May I ask you a favor? I need some tennis balls. Would you please send me a few tennis balls?

We sent tennis balls immediately, of course!

Upplands Vasby Sweden
March 16th 1995

Best Drakke Zimmerman,

This letter is meant to inform you
that the Swedish group of
Amnesty International got the
message from you to EVA ASP.
We are in the process of
acquiring, from Bonn, a
Korean - German dictionary.
Also, the letter was a receipt
that our candy reached
the right addressee.

We are encouraged in our work
for Kim Seong-man to have
and to read all communication
from him to you by the
intermediation of the London
Secretary.

In order to give KSM the right
message, I referred to myself as
a friend of Zimmerman's, which
I'm sure you do not object to.
        Yours very truly Per A Lindberg

Judy Hines, a teacher at Bloomington Junior High School, invited me to speak to her class about Amnesty's work. After my talk, the students wrote to KSM. He was delighted and sent me his thanks.

2/7/97

Dear Drake Zimmerman,

A few days ago I received 9 letters which cute kids at Bloomington Junior High School sent to me. They said that you had told them about me. The lovely letters written by cute kids brought me happiness. I will send a reply letter to Judy Hines in order that she and kids may read my letter. I thank you for telling them about me.

I received your postcard and several packages of undergloves. Hot C mix, Vaseline Intensive Care. It was sweet smelling. And the flavor of the Hot C mix was very good. It was really valuable here. Thanks to you and Bob Connelly I could enjoy it with happiness. I enjoyed it for the first time since imprisonment. Your package always gives me much pleasure. I am grateful to you for your kindness.

Now we have three consecutive holidays of New Year's Day by the lunar calendar. Today is the first day of the holidays. People will enjoy the holidays with joy, but during the period prisoners can't avoid being very bored. Without any program of the day such as physical exercise, meeting visitors, watching TV, etc., we have to stay in our room for three days. I am going to read books and write a lot of letters during the period. New Year's Day by the lunar calendar is the biggest holiday in the year in Korea. People who live away from their hometown come back and spend the holidays at their hometown. Members of a family gather together and share their tender feeling. Ten million people, one fourth of the population of South Korea, are said to have moved toward their hometown for the holidays in this year. Yesterday my friends visited and consoled me who couldn't spend the holidays with my family.

I am deeply grateful to you. Your affection helps me a great deal to take a cheerful view of my life and take heart.

Yours sincerely,

Kim Seong Man

In this letter, KSM tells of exercise, of sounds he can hear and of catching a cold. He writes of being in a community of political prisoners, their concerns and of looking forward to marriage. He says he is 40 years old. By our count, he is only 39, because his birthday is 11 October, 1957. By Korean custom, he is already 40.

3/23/97

Dear Drake Zimmerman,

It is at dawn now. I hear cars running outside the prison. Before breakfast I do always exercise for an hour. I take jogging for about 20 minutes and for the rest of an hour I take breathing exercise. But today I am not going to take exercise. I caught a slight cold. I am lacking in pep.

If a contagious disease prevails in the prison, it is really a big trouble. A contagious disease prevails very quickly in the prison, for many people are crowded in a narrow space. Ten years ago when I was in Seoul prison, dysentery prevailed in the prison. A few patients were reported the first day, several tens of patients were reported the following day, and more than one hundred patients were reported the next day.

There are eight persons in my community—six political prisoners, a warden and a young prisoner whose crime was theft, and has the duty of cleaning. The young prisoner moved into my community three weeks ago, bringing germs of a cold on him. The prisoner passed on his cold to the warden, and the warden passed on his cold to me. I caught a cold after 3-4 years. I am going to take rest and sleep much time all day long except writing and sending you this letter.

I received your many packages with great pleasure. They were Folger's, Wrigley's, Hot C mix and so on. All the things were really of much use here. Whenever I use the things, I feel joy. The things you sent me have been refining my life. I am very pleased that you send me packages often. I am deeply grateful to you.

May I ask you a favor? Would you please include around five cards which are not used into a package next time? I hope to use the cards when I write to my friends in my country or in a foreign country.

I sent a reply letter to Judy Hines this month. She will send my best regards to her cute kids.

I am forty years old. When I was put into prison, I was twenty-eight years old and had no wife and children. At that time I thought it was rather lucky to be a single person, for many prisoners around me were worried about their family affairs—education of their children, chastity of their wives and so on. But I came to my forties, and it makes me lonely not to have a wife and a child. I hope to get married soon after I am released.

Yours sincerely,
Kim Seong Man

The Gum Campaign

One very successful campaign was to send Wrigley's gum to KSM. We often sent 10 or 12 packs of Wrigley's with our letters. The packages were easy to mail and might be a form of currency for him in prison. It was a convenient way to stage a campaign that was easy to execute and provided a very useful item for KSM. Michael O'Reilly of Amnesty in Atlanta helped by putting the notices about our "Stick Up Campaign" in the AI Monthly Mailing to groups. I received e-mails from a couple dozen groups that sent gum.

The gum also helped KSM share with others. KSM wrote that he was happy to be able to offer some gum to his hosts during an annual "day out in society." Every year each Korean prisoner is taken out of prison for a drive and a cup of coffee. The idea is to help keep prisoners in contact with the outside world, albeit for just one day. Kim Song-man seemed to retain the sense of humanity through his entire experience. The gum gave him the means to extend to others a kind gesture despite his being a prisoner.

The warden at one of the later prisons informed KSM that chewing gum was NOT permitted in that prison and would he please tell his friends to quit sending gum! The warden did let him keep the several dozen packs he had already received!

KSM writes of the value of Ivory Soap and being visited by a member of the National Assembly, Korea's congress. He mentions that several acquaintances who were political prisoners now serve in the National Assembly, and that he continues to study German.

96.1.12

Dear Drake Zimmerman,

I received several packages with pleasure which you had sent me in the end of last year and in this year. I received Ivory soap, gum, hand warmer and so on. Ivory soap is of much value. I use it while I am bathing and exchange it for other necessary things. And gum is also of high value here. Most prisoners and I like to chew gum but are not able to purchase it here. I am deeply grateful to you for your warm concern and kindness to send me the precious things which make my life in jail cheerful and happy. My friends, political prisoners here, are envious of me because I often receive packages from foreign countries.

As soon as I moved to Chunju prison, a member of the National Assembly (in whose electoral district Chunju prison is located) visited me. He is my acquaintance. The period when I was in Seoul prison under sentence of death was the peak of Korean Democratization Movement. Many people were restricted at that time. I came to be on intimate terms with many political prisoners. Now four of them have become members of National Assembly and have kept company with me. They sometimes visit me. The member of National Assembly whose electoral district Chunju prison belongs to is one of them. It was very helpful for me that he visited me and asked the authorities of the prison for humane treatment. They take care not to treat me inhumanely.

There is much difference among prisons in respect of facilities. As for Chunju prison we can watch videotapes but we can't use a tape recorder. Chunju prison has no tape recorder for learning foreign languages and we are not obliged to keep a cassette tape recorder. I am going to keep on learning the German language by books.

I thank you for the warm heart and kindness to send me packages of precious things.

Yours sincerely,
Kim Seong Man

KSM had his annual visit outside the prison and was able to share his Wrigley's gum. He writes about desiring "a life of rendering aid" to others and sharing joy with them.

11/6/96

Dear Susan M. Clary,

I received your letter, your picture, my friend, and the package with pleasure. I am deeply grateful to you for your prompt reply.

I like the author, Anthony De Mells. I have read another work of his. I think you really sent me a good friend.

I was very glad to receive your picture. You look courteous and intellectual. I imagined your big smile. I guess you will look kind, beautiful and happy when you make a big smile.

I am 180 cm tall and wear glasses. I am partly bald-headed. My bald head is of heredity nature. I am often said to have an intellectual face.

You said that you would be out of town for a few weeks. What do your cats eat during your long absence?

Do you see Drake Zimmerman quite often in the morning? I owe him a great debt of gratitude. He introduced me to many American friends and made efforts for my release.

I have been outside the prison two weeks ago. I went around here and there with prison officers for five hours outside the prison. It was an annual event of 'learning by observation.' We dropped into a cafe whose name was 'Maison Blanche.' I heard that it was French and meant a white house in English. Tables, sofas and interior decorations were all white in the cafe. A college woman who did a side job in the cafe showed us to a table, took an order and was very kind consistently. I gave her a piece of gum which was in my pocket as a token of gratitude. (It was Wrigley's Winter Fresh which Drake Zimmerman sent me.) I was very happy that she was really grateful to me for the gum.

I want to make a living rendering aid to persons and sharing joy with them. But I have no liberty. I have money which I can hardly spend in the prison and I have few things which I would like to give to others. It was only a piece of gum that I could give the girl as a token of gratitude. I am waiting for my release.

The packages and letters which you have sent me have given me great pleasure. They have been good consolation and encouragement in my hard prison life.

Yours sincerely,
Kim Seong Man

When I heard of KSM's move to Taejeon Prison the first time he was sent there, I wrote letters to the Taejeon Rotary Club, asking them to visit him. This letter followed the Gum Campaign.

1997.7.9

Dear Drake Zimmerman,

Now I am in Taejeon prison. I moved to Taejeon prison in June. I have had much trouble with the authorities here. The trouble caused by unreasonable treatment still exists. I am in bad health now.

I received several tens of letters from USA thanks to the Stick Up Campaign. They gave me consolation and encouragement. They made me forget my loneliness and helped me not to lose self-esteem. They made the burden of the prison life lighter. I know that you suggested the campaign. I thank you from the bottom of my heart.

I came to Taejeon prison by bus of the prison. When only one prisoner moves to another prison, a car is generally used. But a bus was used for me because my burden was a large amount. My burden was mostly books. I have read books for 12 years and have placed one by one in the custody. The books now became a large amount. But for the last 2-3 years I have lived the prison life, giving much more weight to preservation and promotion of my health than to reading.

I have lived in Taejeon prison before. I lived here from 1988.12 — 1992.6. My memory is still vivid that I read your letter for the first time which was sent to Taejeon Rotary Club. A kind member of Taejeon Rotary Club, a warden, showed it to me.

While I was moving to this prison I could see the sight of summer for the first time in a few years. The world was covered with verdant vegetation. It was a magnificent view to me who had seen only some plants which were in the corner of the small playground. Each small hillock looked as if it were an elegant miscellany.

It takes two hours and a half by car from Seoul where my parents live to Taejeon prison. I am pleased that I moved nearer to my home. But whenever I think of the present unreasonable treatment, I still feel unhappy.

The things which prisoners can receive differ from prison to prison. Coffee is not allowed in this prison. I will inquire which items are allowed by packages in this prison, and will tell you in the next letter which items I can receive.

Yours sincerely,
Kim Seong Man

97.7.26

Dear Drake Zimmerman,

A few days ago I received around 10 packages at the same time which you had sent to me. Some of them were transferred to me from Chunju prison, and the others were what you sent to me in Taejeon prison. One of them contained your short letter. Before I received the packages, I had received your card. I am deeply grateful to you for your affection and kindness.

I had hard time for more than one month here in Taejeon prison. I missed my family, my supporters and my friends in a foreign country like you and Bob Connelly. I am gradually recovering from my health.

As soon as I moved to Taejeon prison, I was accommodated with a single room for a mentally deranged prisoner in the structure where I lived. All the rooms in the structure were stuffy and got damp. The wall in my room was mouldy. The clothes and blankets in my room were wet. Using them, my strength gradually declined, and I suffered from a cold all the time for a month.

I moved to a new normal room a few days ago. Now I am recovering my health and am developing my physical strength. A member of the National Assembly will visit me soon to investigate my unreasonable treatment in Taejeon prison.

Your warm concern consoles me and encourages me to keep a hope of the future.

The warden handed over the gum in your packages to me, but he said that he wouldn't next time. Each prison has its characteristic and prisoners are not allowed to chew gum here in Taejeon prison. I hope you to send me several unused cards and very small amount of chocolate in the same package next time.

Yours sincerely,
Kim Seong Man

A Mother's Campaign

Choi In-hwa worked tirelessly for the release of her son, Kim Song-man. In 1992, she went on a round-the-world tour to help win her son's freedom. She wrote on August 3, 1992, "If we fail to free him at this time, we have to wait another 5 years." Unfortunately, her prediction came true; we had to wait those five years.

After writing many letters to us and to others, she devoted herself to visiting KSM and making local connections to get him freed. This section includes some of her letters.

(1992 photograph of Choi In-hwa courtesy of Amnesty International.)

"The most excellent virtue in Korea is to please one's parents and to be respectful and dutiful to them. But I have been in the prison for more than 10 years and have given my parents anxiety and sorrows for a long period. I have a strong will to be dutiful to my old parents and to please them after my release."

— Kim Seong-Man
from a letter to N. Grier Hills 2/11/96

Mr. N. Grier Hills
RR I Box 313
Heyworth, IL 61745 U.S.A.   31 March, 1992

Dear Mr. Hills,

I'm mother of Kim Seong-Man.

My son and I really appreciate your concern and kindness. Many things which you had sent to my son before, reached him in Taejeon prison successfully. But unfortunately it is not allowed to wear a jacket in prison, so he couldn't wear it. As you may know, he can neither receive nor send a letter overseas from prison. Therefore even tho he really wanted to express his thanks to you, you didn't get any response from him. Now on behalf of my son I would like to express deepest appreciation for your kindness and concern. I hope that this is not too late time to express our thanks to you.

During the last a couple of months, We have been very busy to do several works for my son. One of the major works was publishing a book by Kim Seong-Man. The book composed of essays and letters which he had written in prison. Many people have expressed their deep impression after reading the book. Someday in a near future we are going to translate some article of the book into English and will distribute it to many foreign friends in order to deliver my son's deepest thanks.

Recently there have been several news reports about improvement of relationship between south and north Korea. But the news reports do not reflect the reality. We Koreans don't believe that the remarkable improvement will be come true so easily and so fast. Therefore we can't foresee any positive signal that my son will be released soon.

He is still in Taejeon prison. Recently he is maintaining generally good health conditions and he is spending most of his time in reading books. Even tho he can't expect his release in near future, he doesn't feel so lonely. The attentions and considerations from overseas friends like you comfort his prison life.

Looking forward your continuous attention and kindness.

Sincerely,

Choi, In Hwa
Mother of Kim Seong-Man

2 June, 1992

Dear Mr. Zimmerman

The first edition of my son's book was published the end of last November. And this February second edition was printed. But we didn't have enough time, there are several editorial mistake in those two editions. So currently we are trying to fix those errors for revised edition which may be published sometime the end of this year.

It's no problem for us to send several books to you but its mailing cost is so expensive we can't send many copies to you. We are going to send you 5 books via air parcel this weekend. If you need more, we are going to send it via ship. It will takes about 2 months. Please let me know immediately if you need more. He want to translate some article of the book by himself in the prison. But there are quite a lot of limitation, it will be quite difficult. If you have any friend who can read Korean, please ask him to try to translate a article in the book. The article on page 145-186 is worthwhile to translate. If it's not comfortable for your friend, it's quite all right. We will try to translate it in Korea.

The price of the book is 3,600 won. One US $ is equivalent to 790 won. So it costs about US$ 4.5. But we don't want to be paid. Because you are the person who help us so such, it's our great pleasure to present my son's book to you. He also want to give his book to you and other foreign friends who help him. I'll send a copy to my daughter, so you don't have to care about her.

If you get a copy of French television documentary, Please send a copy of it to me. During my visit to Europe. I asked them a copy of it. But I didn't get any action so far. If I can get a copy, I'll try that it can be shown here.

Always thank you so much for your kindness and attention on my son..

sincerely yours

Choi In Hwa, mother of Kim Seong Man

Mr. Drake Zimmerman C.F.P.
PAS(First Affiliated Security) Inc.
1540 E.College Suite 15 A.
Normal, Il.61761, U.S.A.   18 Jun.1991

Dear Sir,

     I'm writing this letter to you as a mother of Kim Seong-
Man in order to express my deepest appreciation for your kindness and attention to my son.

     Kim Seong-Man was very pleased with your attention and
tried to express his thanks to you. But it was not permitted to
send letter to foreign country by the government authority.
Therefore on behalf of himself I would like to convey his real
appreciation to you.

     Even he is still in life imprisonment and Korea government
is getting tighten their control, your kindness and attention
on my son give me a positive hope on his release.

     Recently Kim Seong-Man came to hear about "Paul Harris
Fellow" and he is very interested in the award. If possible,
he want to be nominated and eager to win the honor. I cordially
ask your help for my son's greatest honor. And if there is anything that I can do, please let me know.

     I would like to express my sincere thanks from my heart
to you once again, and look forward to your continuous attention and help to my son's release.

                         Sincerely yours,

                         Choi In-Hwa
                         Mother of Kim Seong-Man

29 June, 1992

Dear Mr. Zimmerman

I'm always thanks for your kindness and attention on my son.
I have received your letter of May 30th. But I couldn't ask him whether he knows Jeewon Lee or not. I'll let you know later. I had sent you 5 copies of the book. Did you received it? If your translator can translate the book into english, please ask him/her translate just a part of the book. (Page 145 through page 186). There are several mistakes in the book he doesn't want to translate all of them. And if your translator finished translation, please let me get a copy of English version. I'll distribute it to other foreign friends.
We have received a copy of video tape about 30 prisoners of conscience from Amnesty International France last week. So you don't have to send it to me. We are going to try to broadcast the film on TV here, we don't think it's easy.
By the way Kim Seong-Man has moved from Taejon to KwangJu prison on June 10th. KwangJu is located in south western part of korea. It takes about 4 hours from Seoul by car. And facilities of the prison is worse than Taejon. We don't know why they make him move. Anyway it's much difficult for me to visit him. The changed address of Kim Seong-Man is as follows;

> Mr. Kim Seong-Man
> #5022 KwangJu Prison
> 88-1 MoonHeung-Dong
> Buk-Gu KwangJu, Korea

Many thanks and regards . . .

sincerely yours

Choi In-Hwa,
mother of Kim Seong-Man

August 3, 1992

Dear Mr. Zimmerman

Thank you so much for your kindness and coordinations for my son.

It's very nice to hear that you have received the books. He thanks very much for all the things which you sent to him. Not all the items are delivered to him all the time. It depends on the situation. Sometimes they deliver the items to him without omission, sometimes they don't. Anyway he enjoys reading books and using useful items like toothbrushes, toothpastes and others. He has his books with him in the prison.

He wrote a short message to you during my last visit to him. Even it's not allowed to write a letter in English, he can write this message during guard's absence. Recently the prisoners of conscience who are in the prisons and many democratic movement organizations went on a demonstration to improve the treatment and environmental conditions of the prisoners. We also joined this demonstration and he stopped eating for 5 days to achieve his objectives. They have accepted most of our request and we stopped demonstration last week. Now he recovered his health condition.

We will have presidential election this coming December. We think this will be the best and last opportunity for his release. If we fail to free him at this time, we have to wait another 5 years. So we are going to organize all the efforts which will be helpful to his release. Therefore I would like to ask your strong attention and support for my son's release. If we set up detail action plan, I'll let you know and ask your active support.

We always thank very much for your kindness and active support.

Sincerely yours,

Choi In-Hwa
Mother of Kim Seong-Man

December 19, 1992

Dear Mr. Grier Hills,

I always thank you for your kindness and affection on my son Kim Seong-Man.

We had presidential election yesterday. Mr. Kim Young Sam has elected as a new president of Republic of Korea for next 5 years. Mr. Kim was one of the most dominant democratic leader throughout his 40 years political career. He resisted against dictatorship to realize democracy in Korea as a leader of opposite party for a couple of decades. But last year, he changed his mind and merged his party with current president Roh Tae Woo's. Therefore we can't expect his democratic policy at this moment.

Kim Seong-Man had commuted from death sentence to life imprisonment in 1988 when Mr. Roh Tae Woo who is current president was elected. In order to show their difference from previous government, new government used to conduct amnesty for the political prisoners. Therefore I think this time will be a very good chance to free my son Kim Seong-Man and many other people who suffer in prison. We are going to ask new president to reconsider the charge against on my son and to free him immediately. We are going to send petition to Mr. Y.S. Kim and other authority members. I would like to ask you to give me a favor sending a letter to new president to ask him to free Kim Seong Man immediately. Your letter will be a great help to free my son. Let me cordially ask your active support to express foreign friends hope for Kim Seong Man's release.

Once again I would like to address that this time will be the best chance to free Kim Seong Man within next 5 years. The amnesty by the new government will be conducted in next January and February time frame. Thank you very much for your kindness.

Sincerely yours,

Choi In-Hwa,
Mother of Kim Seong-Man

August 9, 1993

Dear Mr. Zimmerman:

How are you? I am doing okay. I visited yesterday Kwang ju where my son is. He and other political prisoners just finished hunger strike for a week. They were asking that the annual amnesty on the 15th of August should include all political prisoners this time.

We don't hear yet whether my son will be included under the August 15 amnesty. But, as a result of the strike, my son and other political prisoners at Kwang ju are now allowed to reply directly to abroad, only to individuals who are "not" related to any organizations. You or other concerned AMNESTY people may write to my son directly without saying your relationship to AMNESTY (although you don't say it, my son knows it very well), and then he may reply to you directly.

Despite a political reform since the new president, there are still over 300 political prisoners including my son in South Korea. Please continue to be concerned about my son. We always appreciate your concerns and efforts for my son. I will keep in touch with you. Thank you.

Sincerely,

Choi In-Hwa
(Mother of Kim Seong-man)

"Recently the prisoners of conscience who are in the prisons and many democratic movement organizations went on a demonstration to improve the treatment and environmental conditions of the prisoners. We also joined this demonstration and he stopped eating for 5 days to achieve his objectives. They have accepted most of our request and we stopped demonstration last week."

—From a letter written by Choi In-hwa August 3, 1992

Part Three
Official Correspondence
A Representative Sampling of Official Letters

THE AMBASSADOR
HONG-CHOO HYUN

EMBASSY OF THE REPUBLIC OF KOREA
WASHINGTON, D. C.

Mr. Steven F. Monk
710 South Vermillion Street
Pontiac, Illinois, 61764

November 14, 1991

Dear Mr. Monk:

I am writing in response to a letter I received from Senator Paul Simon in which he asked me to directly inform you on the case of Kim Song-man, who is serving a term of life imprisonment for violating Korea's National Security Law.

While appreciating your personal concern for the Republic of Korea and its citizens, I would like to point out that Mr. Kim's conviction was the result of his violating a long-standing law put in place to ensure the peace and security of my country. Just as the United States has its own Logan Act which prohibits its citizens to have unauthorized contacts with government officials of a hostile country, Korea has security measures to counter the very real threat from North Korea which, among other things, has not given up its obstinate attempt to communize South Korea by means of force.

As I and many observers of Korea agree, under President Roh's leadership, South Korea has taken important strides toward achieving democratic reforms and promoting human rights. In this regard, I am sure that the recent revision of the National Security Law which allowed amnesty for 258 people last May was a vivid testimony of the Korean government's unswerving commitment to advance the principles of democracy and human rights while maintaining vigilance against the subversive threat from North Korea.

As I have already conveyed the concern of some other U.S. citizens on this case to my home government, I will inform you of any new developments.

Sincerely,

Hong-Choo Hyun

First Affiliated Securities, Inc.
Members NASD And SIPC

Ambassador HYUN Hong Joo
Embassy of the Republic of Korea
2370 Massachusetts Avenue, N.W.
Washington, DC 20008   18 December 1991

Your Excellency,   Re: Kim Song-Man

Congratulations on the recent reconciliation pacts signed recently. Would it
now be time to release those prisoners who serve time for the National
Security Act, such as <u>Kim Song-Man</u>? Kim Song Man is being held prisoner in
Taejon Prison, No. 3608. A release for the Holidays or in advance of
President Roe Tae Woo's visit in early January would be greatly appreciated.

As you have seen, many Americans have becoming aware of the situation of
Kim Song-Man and other prisoners like him, and more learn of his situation
daily. The office of the Honorable Senator Paul Simon is keeping me posted
on the progress of Kim Song-Man's case. Other United States Senators are
also interested in Kim Song-Man's fate. I received another letter from
Senator Simon's office again today and they are most happy to help us
further with our efforts to seek Kim Song-Man's release.

I urge you to review Kim Song-Man's case immediately and release him
along with all other political prisoners. Would you please include him in any
general or specific release? <u>Thank you for your review of human rights
cases.</u> I welcome the news of amnesties express hope that all prisoners held
for the peaceful expression of their political views will be released in the
near future. Again, congratulations on the "tide of reconciliation and
cooperation" that has reached your land.

Yours Respectfully and Sincerely,

Drake Zimmerman
Juris Doctor, Chartered Financial Analyst   CC: President ROH Tae Woo
Past President, Rotary Club of Normal, Illinois   Paul Simon, MOC

Drake Zimmerman
Branch Manager	Investment Broker	Registered Principal
P.O. Box 326	1540 E. College, Suite 15A	Normal, IL 61761	(309) 454-7040

(DRAFT of a 1992 letter)

I am writing this letter on behalf of KIM SONG-MAN who is being held as prisoner number 5022 in Kwang Ju Prison. As you are most surely aware, KIM SONG-MAN is being held for speaking in favor of Korean reunification, which is now the official policy of South Korea. I urge you to review his case and seek inclusion in any general or specific release of prisoners held under the General Security Law.

Amnesty International has thoroughly investigated the case of KIM SONG-MAN and found no evidence that he carried out espionage activities or that he used or advocated the use of violence to effect political change. KIM SONG-MAN's continued imprisonment is therefore in violation of the Universal Declaration of Human Rights.

Please let me request you respectfully as newly elected President to free Kim Seong Man as a gesture of goodwill to the international community of those who are interested in promoting democratic reforms throughout the world. At the court KIM said, "The true meaning of reunification (between North and South Korea) is that people with different ideologies can freely interact and travel about in public . . . is it true that only the government can strive for reunification? I too support reunification and cannot sign something which goes counter to reunification. I should walk freely on the street without converting . . ."

I trust that you share my concern regarding the status of KIM SONG-MAN and all "unconverted" political prisoners, and seek their immediate and unconditional release. Thank you very much for allowing me the time to bring this matter to your attention.

Sincerely yours,

Nathan Grier Hills, B.D., M.Div.
Member of Amnesty International Chapter 202
Member of American Civil Liberties Union
Member of Habitat for Humanity International

cc: Korean Ambassador
        U.S. Senator Paul Simon

Embassy of the United States of America
Seoul, Korea

April 4, 1994

Drake Zimmerman
P.O. Box 326
Normal, Illinois 61761

Dear Mr. Zimmerman:

I am writing in response to Senator Paul Simon's March 21 letter to the Ambassador. Senator Simon requested that the Embassy reply directly to you about the case of Kim Song-Man, a former graduate student at Western Illinois University, who is serving a life sentence for violating South Korea's National Security Law.

The Republic of Korea's Ministry of Justice provided the following information about the case.

Begin Text.

Charges: Violation of the National Security Law (NSL)

- While staying in the U.S., Kim Song-Man, guided by North Korean agent Suh Jung Kyun, traveled to Hungary on June 25, 1983. He met with North Korean authorities and received espionage orders from North Korea. On July 4, 1983, he returned to South Korea, organized the group "Chonminjung," and carried out espionage activities.

- On November 16, 1984, Kim traveled to a North Korean safe house in East Berlin. There he joined the North Korean Workers Party, and received espionage training. On December 20, 1984, he returned to South Korea.

Arrest/Trials:

July 30, 1985:   Arrested
January 20, 1986:   Death penalty given by Seoul District Criminal
                      Court

May 31, 1986:	Seoul High Court rejected appeal.
September 23, 1986:	Supreme Court turned down appeal; sentence finalized
December 21, 1988:	Sentence commuted to life in prison

End text.

Human rights is a fundamental American principle which the Department of State supports throughout the world. The Korean government is aware of our views on human rights issues such as the National Security Law.

I hope this information is of use. A copy of this letter also has been sent directly to Senator Simon's office in Washington.

Sincerely,

Mark Minton
Minister Counselor for
Political Affairs
American Embassy, Seoul, Korea

United States Department of State

Washington, D.C. 20520

July 20, 1995

Mr. Robert Connelly
1404 N. Fell
Bloomington, IL 61701

Dear Mr. Connelly:

This is in response to your letter of April 9, 1995 to
the office of Senator Paul Simon, concerning the imprisonment
of Kim Song-Man. Senator Simon's office has requested that
the State Department respond directly to your concerns. This
is an interim reply to your request; we have asked our
Embassy in Seoul to look into the particulars of Mr. Kim's
imprisonment and will report back to you with any information
it is able to provide.

Please do not hesitate to contact us if you have further
questions.

Sincerely,

David E. Brown
Director
Office of Korean Affairs

cc: Office of Sen. Paul Simon

Part Four

Lighting Up the Dark Days
Of penguins, prison conditions and prayers

As you read the letters, you can understand the real reason we wanted to compile this book: To share Kim Song-man's letters to us. We found his letters so touching, so poignant, that we HAD to share them. The letters reveal a deep and broad understanding of humanity, of lives touched by the actions of others.

Kim Song-man offered more than just a description of his daily existence in the prisons of South Korea. His responses to our letters were by turns serene, melancholy, and amusing as he related prison anecdotes. His observations on the world and its people, and his own struggle with loneliness and hope are especially insightful.

3/23/95

Dear Drake Zimmerman,

Spring has come. The high wall of the prison hinders me from seeing mountains and trees of spring, but I can find a part of spring by
soft beams of sunlight in exercise time.

How is it going in this spring? How is Jan Elfline? Is Malaria
Project going well? I think many people are being given relief thanks
to Malaria Project. I have a dream to make a contribution to
mankind someday like you.

In these days I learn the Japanese language as well as the German
language. I learned Japanese in the prison around 9 years ago when
I was a prisoner under sentence of death. At that time I learned
Japanese intensively not to use the language afterwards but to
indulge in the pleasure of learning a language and to let lingering
attachment to the land of the living pass from my mind, learning a
language. The more sorrowful I was for lingering attachment, the
harder I studied the language. Owing to the study, I have no difficulty in reading, writing, and speaking Japanese. Fortunately, in
Taegu prison political prisoners are often able to take advantage of
audiovisual facilities to learn foreign languages. Learning Japanese
and German brings me at present not only pleasure of study but the
feeling of worth, for not being a prisoner under sentence of death I
can use the language afterwards in my life.

I wear glasses. About a week ago I went to an ophthalmic hospital outside the prison to have new glasses made. The new glasses
were O.K. and now I wear them. In the hospital I stood in front of an
oculist, wearing a prisoner's clothes, being handcuffed, and being
bound with a rope. The oculist was a slender lady and seemed to be
around 30 years old. Maybe she took me for a thief who had a strong
physique. Otherwise, as I look a little intellectual, she may have
taken me for a swindler. She gave me a cold welcome and showed me
a distant manner. She hesitated to talk with me and was unwilling
to make an explanation. She made me sad. On my way to the prison
I decided that I would not have a prejudice against a man of humbleness and would be affectionate and kind to him.

Yours sincerely,
Kim Seong Man
P.s. Now I heard that three tennis balls from you and a postcard
from David W. Babson had just arrived at the prison. They will be
delivered to me soon. Thank you very much!

Of rats and cats... Along with rats, cats and sounds in the night, KSM dreams of an active, productive life. Clare McVey was Amnesty International's East Asia coordinator and a great help to Kim Song-man's case. Clare helped to arrange an around-the-world trip for KSM's mother. His mention of the article made us wonder about how lax the censorship was in the prison! We soon found out. His next letter offers a real surprise in terms of what KSM was allowed to see while in prison!

6/24/95

Dear Malcolm Purves,

I received the package with pleasure. All the items in the package were very useful to me and I was very pleased.

I moved to a new room a few days ago. I was very busy in these days repairing the room. I covered the floor of the room with laminated paper to stop up rat holes and chinks. There are many rats under every floor of these rooms. Sleeping in the night, I can often hear sounds which rats are making under the floor. Scratching something, or running and playing. There are lots of rats in the prison. The reason why there are so many rats in the prison is that leftovers of food are scattered here and there in the prison. To breed animals privately is strictly forbidden in the prison. But to breed cats is an exception, because cats are expected to catch rats. But they are not up to the expectation. They don't catch rats. There are enough leftovers I think that leftover food is more delicious than rats to cats. If we catch a rat and bring it to a cat, she has no interest in it and is not willing to touch it. If the rat jumps at her bravely, she feels annoyed and goes away.

I am 38 years old. I think I can lead an active life in a society for about 30 years in future. The imagination of my future in which I will realize my dream brings me pleasure and physical health. Your encouragement also gives me strength. I always feel grateful to you.

Do you know the lady in London, Clare McVey? I have recently read an article of her interview in a Korean magazine.

Yours sincerely,
Kim Seong Man

9/23/95

Dear Drake Zimmerman,

As my memory runs, your birthday is October 8. I wish you many happy returns of the day. I hope that a New Year will bring you much pleasure.

My younger sister visited me last month. I was told that she had talked with you for an hour on the telephone. I thank you for your kindness to talk with my sister for a long time in the middle of the day.

We had Independence Day of Korea last month. The day is in memory of August 15, 1945 when our country was liberated from Japanese Imperialists. The government grants a particular pardon and releases prisoners on August 15 every year in honor of the national independence. Many political prisoners expected to be released on the day. But no more than a small minority of 5% was liberated. In comparison with the previous government the present on has a weaker will to grant an Amnesty to political prisoners. As long as the present policy of human rights of Korea maintains, I can't have a bright outlook to be released under the present government. I think I am now in the period of darkness. But I will endure this darkness well. I will stand this darkness, keeping my health and accomplishing spiritual growth.

I have often received you packages such as a headband, Ivory soap, and a book of German words and so on. I am very sorry not to send you a letter of gratitude. Ivory soap which you sent me was very useful. Have you seen the movie, "The Shawshank Redemption?" I saw it here by a video tape recorder. Such common things as a small hammer or a piece of cigarette are precious and high-priced in Shawshank prison. A small hammer is to Shawshank prison what Ivory soap from a foreign country is to Taegu prison. I want to receive some more Ivory soap from a foreign country.

Yours sincerely,
Kim Seong Man

P.s. Steven F. Monk often sends me postcards. Please give my best regards.

Kim Song-man speaks of his religion and his enjoyment of singing in a gospel song contest with his fellow prisoners.

10/2/95

Dear David W. Babson,

I was glad to receive your letter. I appreciate your kind concern.

Today is October 2. The sky of the autumn in Korea is high and blue. The weather is neither warm nor cold. The weather in these days is the best to the prisoners. I live calmly keeping a peaceful mind.

My mother is a daughter of a clergyman. I and my brother and sisters were brought up in the atmosphere of Christianity. I have gone to church from the time I was a child. But it is a few years since I came to be enthusiastic in Christian faith. I have made efforts to strengthen my faith. A few days ago I took part in a sacred gospel song contest in Taeju prison. I chose the song of a pilgrim which was my favorite song. I and my two friends who were political prisoners sang it as a musical trio. We had smart practice, and made much endeavor to make a beautiful chord. When the results of the contest were announced, we were uneasy. But we won the second prize among eleven teams. I was much contented with the second prize. The participation in the contest will become a happy memory in my life.

Now I continue to study Japanese and German. It is not difficult for me to speak Japanese and read Japanese books, but it is not easy to listen to Japanese. I practice to listen to Japanese intensively with a cassette player. I am not proficient in German yet. I can get enough texts of the Japanese and German books. I appreciate your suggestion to send me those books, but I can get them here.

I have often received your postcards with pictures of trains. I am deeply grateful to you for your warm and sustaining concern. I hope you to make a happy life in beautiful weather of the autumn.

Yours sincerely,
Kim Seong-man

11/4/95

Dear Malcolm Purves,

The sky of autumn in Korea is high and blue. The weather is not cold yet in these days. But winter will come soon. Winter in Taeju is colder than that of other regions in Korea.

Prisoners' rooms have no heating system and the bitter cold in winter will often cause pain to prisoners. I was given a nickname of a penguin last winter. I warmed myself with thick clothes and became fat to bear the bitter cold last winter. My friends nicknamed me a penguin and they greeted me in the morning, saying 'Good morning, Mr. Penguin.' I am going to become a penguin this winter, too.

Prisoners dislike the bitter cold, but we have an advantage in winter. The advantage is to be able to make some food for ourselves. A briquette stove will be set up on the passageway in winter. We can bake bread, fry eggs, and make stew soup using the fire in the stove. To use the fire to make food is illegal, but we do. In these days we talk with expectations about the food which we can make using the briquette stove.

Am in good health and make a peaceful life.

I am deeply grateful to you for your warm concern and effort for my release.

Yours sincerely,
Kim Seong Man

KSM is moved to yet another prison and is relieved to find he has a flush toilet again. Oh, the small pleasures of life: plumbing and heat!

12/8/95

Dear Drake Zimmerman,

I was very glad to receive your letter of 11/8/95. It was the first letter of yours in this year. I was very pleased to see your handwriting, which was very familiar to me.

I moved to a new prison on Nov. 29. The new prison named Chunju prison is nearer to my house than the former prison. It takes about 3 hours from my house to the new prison. I am pleased that it will be less hard for my parents to come here by car who are over seventy years old.

Before I left the former prison, I expected to see the scenery outside the prison. I wanted to see mountains, plains and bustling streets. But it was really regrettable that I couldn't see out of the window while I was moving to a new prison by bus because the window was covered with iron.

I live in a single room in Chunju prison, too. The room is a little larger than that of the former prison. I am pleased that my room has a flush toilet. A flush toilet is very important to prisoners' sanitation. I live in a building in which only political prisoners live. Generally speaking, we can get either treatment when we live in a building where only political prisoners live.

What you wrote about "attitude" made a deep impression on me. And I agree with you. I am going to think over my attitude carefully from now on, before I make a decision. I will make an effort to have an attitude which will draw good result.

I am grateful to you for your warm concern and encouragement.

Yours sincerely,
Kim Seong Man

96.1.28

Dear Isabelle Vonhoff

I received a package and a card which you had sent me on January 1. I and my friends here had with relish what you had sent me. We had a good time of it. My friends say Hello to you. I thank you for the good present.

Yesterday I received lots of letters and cards from Taeju prison after I left the prison. Among them there were cards from Malcolm Purves and Claude Kilbert. A picture was enclosed in the card from Malcolm Purves. The picture was said to have been taken at his wedding. He was in traditional Scottish costume and wore a skirt. He told me that he had been informed by you of the fact that I didn't have his picture. I thank you for informing him.

There were 3 penguins on the card from Malcolm Purves. I am often called 'Mr. Penguin' in winter for I look fat in winter for thick clothes. Malcolm Purves sent 3 friends to Mr. Penguin who is lonely. I will send him a reply soon.

It is regrettable that I can't play tennis at Chunju prison. But comparing to other prisons it is beneficial that we are supplied with hot water abundantly. I pour hot water in a big water bucket when I sleep. Then it isn't cold in the blankets. The bucket with hot water is invaluable thing in my room which has no heating system at all.

Yours sincerely,
Kim Seong Man

2/11/96

Dear N. G. Hills,

Recently I received your Christmas card a Chunju prison which you had sent to Taeju prison. It arrived at Taegu prison after I left there. I remember your name well. You sent me packages many times. But it was not until I received the card that I knew the fact that you were 81 years old.

I think that you have learned lots of lessons through your long life. They would be precious and valuable to the young. How happy I would be if you were my grandfather! If so, I could be taught wisdom and instruction by you. They would be another light on my way of my life.

Is your daily life happy? I wonder what you do every day. My father is 74 years old and my mother is 69 years old. My father had his waist operated on a few months ago and he is not healthy now. The most excellent virtue in Korea is to please one's parents and to be respectful and dutiful to them. But I have been in the prison for more than 10 years and have given my parents anxiety and sorrows for a long period. I have a strong will to be dutiful to my old parents and to please them after my release.

I am grateful to you for your kindness and warm concern.

Yours sincerely,
Kim Seong-Man

2/12/96

Dear Malcolm Purves,

I received with pleasure at Chunju prison your package and card
which you had sent to Taeju prison. Your package of socks, soap and
gum was of much use. It was very helpful. And I received also a card
which contained your picture and 3 penguins. I really wanted to keep
your picture. And I was very delightful to find 3 penguins on your
card. Thank you for sending 3 friends to 'Mr. Penguin.'

There are only political prisoners in the building where I am. All
of us use a single room respectively. Do you know the fact that most
of political prisoners who have used a single room for a long time are
somewhat nervous? They are apt to have misunderstanding and pick
up a quarrel with others. Troubles in human relations bring on
stress. One's stress in jail has a bad and direct influence upon his
physical health. A political prisoner is exposed to stress which
emerges from two directions. One direction is from the comrades,
political prisoners, and the other direction is from guards of the prison. Their unreasonable order brings prisoners stress. I make a daily
effort to live cheerfully and happily. Long period's experience in jail
has taught me how to avoid stress and how to lesson or overcome
stress. I endeavor to live cheerfully everyday for my mental and
physical health.

Yours sincerely,
Kim Seong Man

Feb. 29, 1996

Dear Drake Zimmerman,

Spring is coming. The weather in Korea is still cold. The temperature drops as low as −5 degrees C in the morning. But sunbeams get
brighter and are gradually changing into soft and warm sunlight of
spring.

I received your letter and a book. I am deeply grateful to you and
Jan for the help to talk about me in the seminar and to write various
officials letters. Your packages are very helpful to my life in jail.

Steven F. Monk sometimes sends me postcards. The pictures on the postcards are very beautiful. The postcards take me to the beautiful scenery and bring me pleasure. Would you please send my best regards to Steven F. Monk?

I recently received letters from Susan M. Clary and Mrs. Patricia Madden. I heard that you had introduced me to them. Susan M. Clary sent me a long letter of kindness and sincerity. I will send them letters soon.

Letters have often been sent to me by Julie Boswell for a few years. I guess you know her. Does she work at your office? I am still in the dark about her. She doesn't write her address on an envelope at all times. Send my best regards if you know her.

One of the most important things in jail is to keep a good friendship with other political prisoners. Once a prisoner falls out with another prisoner and their personal relations have become irreconcilable, it brings lots of mental pains to them. It is impossible to forget each other, because there are only several prisoners in a community. With ill feeling they cannot help seeing each other, conversing with each other on a subject and taking exercise together every day. Once a prisoner becomes estranged seriously from another prisoner, it does much harm to his mental and physical health.

I have endeavored to have more generosity to a defect in other political prisoner's character for a long time. I have been led to more generosity to others by reading books of mental hygiene and psychoneurosis, my bitter experience due to my impatience and lack of generosity, and careful penetration into ups and downs of my feelings. I cannot but go on putting forth efforts to be more generous till I will be released.

Yours sincerely,
Kim Seong Man

P.s. 1. The picture of Mahatma Gandhi inspired me. I thank you and Jan from the bottom of my heart.

2. I and my friends here have come to like Wrigley's Spearmint very much. My friends here say hello to you in gratitude. Would you please send it to me often?

3. May I ask you to use a little larger envelope than a letter envelope when you send me a package? A package of a letter envelope is liable to be lost in the prison after it arrived at the prison safely.

Mar. 1, 1996

Dear David W. Babson,

Now we have the holiday of the anniversary of Independence
Movement of March 1st. On a holiday we can't take daily exercise on
a playground, and can't meet visitors. We have to stay in our rooms
all day long. People in society enjoy a holiday, but prisoners in jail are
bored on a holiday.

Spring has come. Last winter we had the coldest weather that we
had had for 10 years in Korea. I was able to stand the cold thanks to
hot water. I poured hot water into water pails. I held a water pail in
my bosom by day as well as by night. Last winter I didn't lose my
health and never caught a cold.

Now spring has come. Sunbeams are soft and bright. It is much to
be regretted that I can't see trees and flowers at all around me. Out
of the window in my room can I see no more than a sky and a wall
which is very near to my room. The sky is narrow and cracked by iron
bars. On the playground which is attached to the structure where I
live, I can see only a sky, a high wall and some water tanks which are
placed on the rooftop of an apartment building.

I and my friends here will sow seeds of a sunplant, a sunflower and
so on in the corner of the playground in this spring. They will be the
only plants that we can see here.

The package of ivory soap which your sent me by sea mail arrived
safely. I am deeply grateful to you for your warm concern and kindness. I am in good health. I was very weak in my childhood and did-
n't like to take exercise. I was a very poor player in games. After
imprisonment I was given an hour to take exercise every day except
Sundays and holidays. I couldn't but be earnest in exercise to keep
my physical health. I have played basketball, soccer and soon for
more than 10 years. Now I am not a poor player. Yesterday I and my
friends here had a basketball game against younger prisoners. My
team won. I was of good help to the victory. Now I am very pleased
that I am not a poor player in games like in society.

I hope that your wish to be in graduate school again will come true
this year.

Yours sincerely,
Kim Seong-man

April 24, 1996

Dear Drake Zimmerman,

I had my hair cut in the barbershop of the prison yesterday. Those who cut prisoners' hair are also prisoners. While a prisoner was cutting my hair, the head of the security department entered the barbershop. He was making a round of the whole prison. He has the substantial power and prisoners feel uneasy and are puzzled in his presence. He entered the barbershop and found me. He walked up to me and watched the prisoner cutting my hair. The head treats me with a warm heart in ordinary times. He asked the prisoner to cut my hair charming and watched for a few minutes. But the prisoner was much embarrassed and was at a loss to know what to do. I was anxious lest he should make my hair be in bad shape. The prisoner, who was on pins and needles, cut no more than a place of my hair all the time while the head watched him cutting my hair. When the head had gone out of the barbershop, there was little hair on the left part of my head. I drew a long breath. It was inevitable for him to cut almost all hair on my head.

Patricia Madden sent me a package. I think you informed her what items would be useful to me. I thank you very much. As well as Ivory soap, she sent me "Wrigley's" and "Hershey's" I am prohibited from writing the list of what I had with relish in the letter. So I enumerated the manufacturing company instead. Her package was of much use.

I got a letter from Julie Boswell. She wrote her address on the front of the envelope for the first time. I think you told her. I thank you very much. I will send her a reply soon.

At Chunju prison I can receive as many letters from foreign countries as foreigners send to me, but I am allowed to write a letter to a foreigner once per 7-10 days. When I receive two letters from foreign countries at a time, I can write a prompt reply letter only to one person.

Thanks to you, I can receive many letters and packages from Americans. Those letters and packages give me great pleasure and give vitality to my lonely life. I really want to thank you for your great concern and affection that you have introduced your friends to me.

I and my friends are deeply grateful to you. And I hope you to continue to send me "Wrigley's."

Yours sincerely,
Kim Seong Man

The support we received from AI/USA Korea Cogroup coordinators Ed Baker and Mike Dodd really helped keep the members of our Adoption Group going over the years.

In a letter dated March 18, 1996, Mike Dodd acknowledged the receipt of copies of some of the letters we received from Kim Song-man. He echoed our own sadness at reading of KSM's loneliness in prison and his desire for a "normal lifestyle" and family.

Mike also remarked on the fact that our prisoner always shared things we sent him with those around him, noting that it reflected "...the great spirit of sharing and generosity in the Korean people..."

"I and my friends here have come to like Wrigley's Spearmint very much. My friends here say hello to you in gratitude."

—KSM in a letter to Drake Zimmerman, February 29, 1996

Part Five

Toward Release

"… Kim Song-man spent almost three years under sentence of death, until his sentence was commuted to life imprisonment. It was further reduced to 20 years' imprisonment in the March 1998 prisoner amnesty. Amnesty International believes he should now be released."

From an Amnesty International report on South Korean long-term prisoners still held under the National Security Law May 1998

The Increasing Buoyancy

Over the years KSM's letters seemed more and more buoyant in tone, nearly spiritual. They reflected what appeared to be clear contact with the deeper meaning of his life, of conscious, chosen control over his attitude. He mentioned that having faced death was a tremendous gift to him. He could never take certain aspects of life or human contact for granted again. Once again, Kim Song-man inspired us all.

6/14/96

Dear David W. Babson,

It is summer here. The temperature is around 30 degrees C every-day. When I take exercise in the playground, I feel the skin of my back smart a little under the sun's rays. My room is on the first floor of the two-storied structure and I feel less warm in my room than out-side. The sunplants on the playground are growing well.

I received your letter and package with pleasure. I received maps with interest. Ivory soap and Wrigley's are of much use here. I feel grateful to you for your warm kindness to send me the package. My friends in the community are thankful to you, too.

I congratulate you on being accepted to begin Ph.D. studies at Syracuse University. I am sure that you will become a genuine and sincere scholar. I am very happy to hear that you look forward to write a dissertation on the archaeology of the two aspects of Ameri-can agriculture and rural society which you have wanted to write.

Now I correspond with a girl who is totally paralyzed. She majored in dancing before. When she was a senior, she encountered a car acci-dent and got total paralysis which was incurable. She has a normal function above her neck—her brain, eyes, nose, ears, and mouth. She recovered some function of the fingers after a few years of desperate efforts. I feel sad when I remember her condition to live being total-ly paralyzed. I correspond with her to be her kind companion to chat with her and to console her well. In 1986 I got an irrevocable judge-ment of death sentence and was under sentence of death for two years and four months. Execution of a death sentence will happen at any time except holidays. I didn't know when I would be hanged. It could be tomorrow, the day after tomorrow or today. It gave me bit-ter grief to be separated from my dear family and the world and to leave my work in my youth. I lived in deep sorrow in the long peri-od.

After that period I came to gain a better understanding of others who suffer great misfortune. I understand their thought well and nod my head, hearing what they express. I am familiar with the sub-jects they would like to discuss. I sent her a letter and now wait for her reply. Our correspondence will bring our lives more philosophi-cal speculation and more sincere attitude toward our lives.

I think you feel a little sad to leave your friends, your house and beautiful flowers. I hope you will be in good health during your stay in New York which will advance your career.

Yours Sincerely,
Kim Seong-man

1996.7.15

Dear Drake Zimmerman,

When I was a middle school boy, I read Albert Einstein's essay. He said that most people who made efforts for human welfare came to be disappointed at man's egoistic mind and lose their volition. And he said that he was one of a few persons who were not disappointed at man's egoistic mind and continued to keep enthusiastic and self-sacrificing attitude.

Reading Albert Einstein's essay at that time, I couldn't believe that man was so self-interested. And I was much surprised to hear that there were only a few persons who accepted man's egoistic mind with magnanimity and continued to keep self-sacrificing attitude for human welfare.

Now I am 39 years old and came to know that Albert Einstein's opinion had not been so incorrect that men were self-interested. Now I agree that persons who make devotional efforts for human welfare are apt to lose their volition in the face of man's egoistic mind.

It is clearly a matter for joy to win admiration of others. But I think one has a weak basis if his attitude is swayed by others' admiration, criticism or egoistic mind. I think god's praise and consolation are the only valuable thing. As for me, I take heart from dialogue with god.

I guess that you have sometimes been faced with man's egoistic mind, and been disappointed, pushing the Malaria Project forward. I think the fact that you have carried out the Malaria Project untiringly for a few years proves you great personality that you have overcome the disappointment and preserved your self-sacrificing attitude for human welfare.

I respect you. Owing to your personality many people didn't lose their lives and enjoy their valuable lives. I will pray god to give you consolation, praise and encouragement.

The Neuro Linguistic Programming (NLP) book which you sent me was very instructive. I make much of it. And the visualizations are very useful to me in jail, true to your expectations. When someone makes me get angry or feel sad, I can look at the situation more objectively through visualizations. My anger or sorrow which is caused by my thought, "How dare he speak to me like that?" or "How dare he behave such way?" is remarkably weakened with the help of visualizations. And then I come to have a changed thought that he is one of many persons who speak like that and behave such way. I am deeply grateful to you for sending me the good book.

(continued on next page)

(continued from previous page)

I look at the world map every day. It doesn't make my spirit fall asleep, and makes me keep my hopes up.

Yours sincerely,
Kim Seong Man

9/1/96

Dear Drake Zimmerman,

I am in better health at Chunju prison than I was at any other prison. I take exercise for an hour before breakfast everyday. I practice gymnastics and jogging. They refresh my body and mind and make me be in vigor till I go to bed. In these days new hair has appeared and grown on the region of my bald head. I think my good health and peaceful mind enable new hair to show up and grow. Nowadays it is very amusing to look in a mirror to see the length of my new hair.

I have read a book "Real Love" written by Theodore Isaac Rubin for a few days. He says that real love transmutes our life in a pleasant thing and makes sufferings in our life endurable. Real love is said to treat or lessen our stress, uneasiness and melancholy and lengthen our life.

I think it is in jail that we need real love very much. Under our given condition, it is not easy for us to have and develop real love fruitfully.

On the other hand I can have and feel real love through visitors and persons who correspond with me. You are one of my best friends. I appreciate your kindness and sincerity. By my reading of the book I came to know that my appreciation and real love, which you have brought to me, were precious in my life, and were very helpful to my health. And I know that thanks to you, I could form a friendship and keep a good company with Bob Connelly, David W. Babson, Susan M. Clary and other friends. I always feel grateful to you.

Yours sincerely,
Kim Seong Man

11/16/96

Dear Drake Zimmerman,

Winter is coming. In winter I warm myself with thick clothes, for we have no heating system in a room. I love my neckcloth and my cap made of cloth. When I wear a neckcloth, I feel happy without knowing why. And I enjoy wearing a cap, for it covers my bald head. Having a cap on, I am often said to look handsome.

Susan M. Clary sometimes sends me a letter and a package. Maybe she is now on the road and out of town. She told me that she went to a shop in the morning for coffee and often found you. She told me about your favorable impression and spoke in high terms of you. I am deeply grateful to you for introducing the sincere and kind lady to me.

I hope you received the birthday card and the letter which I had sent to you at the end of September. I had my 40th birthday on 10 October. The age of forty is said to be the age of "BULHOK" (No Doubt) in Korea. "BULHOK" means to have an insight into matters of life and to have no doubt. But as for me there are too many lessons and truths I have to learn.

I read the Proverbs in the Old Testament of the Bible on my birthday every year. Every year I make up my mind on my birthday to make a living according to the instruction and wisdom which God taught me in the Proverbs. I read it in this year, too. As for me it is an invaluable treasure.

Yours sincerely,
Kim Seong Man

12/8/96

Dear Helen Prince,

I thank you for your Christmas card of 11/13. I remember that you have written to me. I am sorry that I didn't send you a reply letter. It is not easy for me to get a new foreigner. But it is comparatively easy to send a letter of gratitude to a person who sent me a package. I will send you a letter after I receive the package which you mentioned in your card.

I am very glad to hear that you live in a place which is not far from Western Illinois University. Your card carried my thoughts back to the happy memories in Macomb.

I am deeply grateful to you from the bottom of my heart for your warm concern and kindness. And I hope you to send my best regards to your friends.

I wish you a very happy holiday season and I wish you a happy New Year.

Kim Seong Man

In the next letter, KSM longs for Folgers coffee and a unified Korea. His determination to unify South and North Korea earned KSM the death penalty, torture and imprisonment. That he can still utter the words shows what guts and willpower this man has!

9/25/96

Dear Drake Zimmerman,

A week ago a member of the National Assembly and my mother visited me. He and I attended the same university, and he is my senior by two years. In college days, we devoted ourselves to anti-dictatorship movement together. He was elected to the National Assembly last April. We were very pleased to see each other after a long time. He induced me to establish a business after release. He expressed his opinion that it would be better for me to engage in business than politics or social movement because the fact that I made contact with North Korean communists would be a handicap in an anti-Communist state, South Korea, even though I am not a communist. I didn't agree to his proposal. I will make efforts to unify South and North Korea after my release and I wish to work in an international organization in my distant future.

The senior is a member of an opposition party. We have a presidential election in December, next year. I expect a change of regime. I think that if an opposition party comes into power, I will be liberated.

May I ask you a favor? I hope you to send me the same "Folgers" as Bob Connelly sent me. He sent me two kinds. Anyone is O.K. It is of great help to my health. It helps digestion and makes me become high-spirited. It is very necessary for my health; we can't get such table luxuries at all in the prison.

I celebrate your birthday. I hope you to enjoy much pleasure on your birthday.

Yours sincerely,

Kim Seong Man

3/29/97

Dear Susan M. Clary

With great pleasure did I receive your letter of 3/10/97. I am very sorry not to have sent you a letter for a long time. Was your trip to Reno, Nevada pleasant? How was your dearest friend in Reno? Did you have a good time of it there?

I am forty years old. I was imprisoned in my age of 28, and have lived in prison for about twelve years. I think I have turned the turning point of my whole life. It makes us sad to be mortal. I have thought over for many years why God gave man the destiny of death. I don't know why. Why do you think God gave us the destiny of death?

It was much to be regretted that I heard you had had breast cancer two years ago. I hope you will heal completely.

After I was sentenced to death, the sky looked bluer and the world looked much more beautiful than before. I really had a different appreciation for things. The different appreciation which I had under sentence of death has hardly been changed after commutation and it is now my valuable property.

All the things which you sent me were really precious and very useful here. I remember that you sent me a Post It Note before. It was of much use here. Would you please include a few Post Its, when you send me a package next time?

Yours Sincerely,
Kim Seong Man

KSM was able to send this letter to Clare McVey at Amnesty International Headquarters.

Dear Clare Mcvey   12/8/96
I was very happy to find your picture in the magazine of mall. And I was very pleased to know much about you. I read in the magazine that my letter ~~was sent~~ had been read in a general assembly. I thank you.
I wish you a very happy holiday season and a happy New Year.
My best wishes.

Yours sincerely

새해에는 더욱 건강하시고
모든 소망 이루시기 바랍니다.

With Best Wishes for
the Holidays and the Coming Year

보내는사람 Kim Seong Man
Chunbuk - Do
Chunju P.O. Box. No 72-2035
Chunju Prison
Republic of Korea

Via Airmail

Miss Clare Mcvey
1 Easton Street London
WC1X 8DJ U.K.

KSM helps to resolve conflict, even while he is in prison.

97.4.27

Dear Drake Zimmerman,

About 10 days ago I received the unused cards which you had sent me. I thank you for the cards. They are really very useful.

There are less than twenty political prisoners in Chunju prison. I am the representative of them. When trouble happens, I confer with the authorities of the prison. I am trusted by the political prisoners. Besides Chunju prison, I experienced five other prisons and in my prison life of twelve years, I have been a representative of political prisoners for about seven years.

I, as a representative, have not been distrusted by my colleagues. I have been faithful to duty and loyal to them. But in my early years after I became a representative, I and my colleagues often struggled with the authorities of the prison. It was partly due to our unskillfulness to solve a problem depending on struggle rather than on skillful human relations. In Chunju prison we have solved problems by skillful conference and enjoy the peace between political prisoners and the authorities of the prison. The peace is essential to our mental and physical health.

Our power in negotiation with the authorities of the prison is derived from individuals and organizations outside the prison. Readiness of organizations, members of the National Assembly and individuals to assist prisoners of conscience at any moment is the pressure to the authorities of the prison and is directly our strength. Without their assistance, our strength is no better than that of general prisoners.

Five years ago four elders of my intimate acquaintances were elected as members of the National Assembly. Last year one of them lost the election and two more friends were newly elected. Now I have five intimate acquaintances who are members of the National Assembly. I am in constant correspondence with them and they sometimes visit me. It was not until my friends of members of the National Assembly began to visit me that I was treated reasonably and earnestly by the authorities of the prison.

The authorities of Chunju prison want to be on good terms with me. In Chunju prison I and my colleagues get along with the authorities in peace. We think highly of peace.

Yours sincerely,
Kim Seong Man

1997.5.8.

Dear Helen Prince,

I received your letter and pictures with great pleasure. I thank
you for sending them. The article of the developer of the snack food
was very interesting. I was very glad to see you and your husband in
the picture. You and your husband look younger than your age. You
have golden hair. My hair is black. All Koreans have black hair. The
black hair becomes white, getting years of age. My mother has white
hair. I have a question. Doesn't the color of golden hair change? You
still have beautiful golden hair.

You said that when you returned, you would begin serving on the
Board of the United Nations Association in Bloomington. I have an
interest in your future work. What kind of work will you do in the
United Nations Association? And may I ask which occupation you are
engaged in?

The fifth wheel in the picture was really very big. It was as good
as a small house. I saw the picture with my friends. I explained the
fifth wheel to my friends. I thank you for sending me the pictures and
explaining them to me.

Your warm concern gives me much pleasure. It is good consolation
and encouragement in my hard prison life.

Yours Sincerely
Kim Seong-Man

1997.6.4

Dear Marie Anne De Rue,

I received your letters two times with great pleasure.

With deep interest did I read your letters introducing yourself and explaining the way of your life. I wanted to send you a reply letter immediately, but it was a little difficult to get permission to send a letter to a new person in a foreign country. Now I got permission to correspond with you, and I am happy. Which language do you speak in your country? Is it French?

And I have one more question. What does De Rue mean in your name? Is it your family name? A few days ago I received a package from Kilbert Claude who is Roland's friend. I will send him a card of thanks soon. You said that you met Roland Ginter at Isabelle's home. All of them are my friends. I have their pictures I know their features. How about sending me a picture? If you don't mind, I hope to keep your picture.

I love to see flowers. But I can hardly see flowers somewhere about here. My sight is hindered by other structures or the high wall of the prison. There is a small playground which is attached to the structure where I live. It is smaller than a tennis court. I take exercise there for an hour everyday.

Some plants for food are growing in the corner of the playground. They are lettuce, crown daisies and leeks. Their leaves are still small and narrow, but we can't wait for them to grow bigger. Whenever pork is distributed in the prison, we pluck them and mix them with pork and boiled rice. We make rice hash. It is very delicious. We are now waiting for the rain which will make the leaves grow fast.

When I got to the playground in this morning, the sky was partly overspread with dark clouds. But the clouds were rather fine and the plants in the corner of the playground were animated. I felt refreshed seeing the clouds and the plants. I felt happy without knowing why. Only a man who is alive can have euphoria. After going through the bitter period of 2 years and 4 months when I was a prisoner under sentence of death, I sometimes feel happy, realizing that I am alive.

Yours sincerely
Kim Seong Man

July 1997

Dear Marie Anne De Rue,

I moved to Taejeon prison last month. The package which you sent to Chunju prison was transferred to me in Taejeon prison. And I received your letter, two pictures and the things a week ago. I am deeply grateful to you for your kindness to send them. The things in the package were of much use, and I had chocolate and sweets with relish. The T-shirt was nice, too. When my mother visited me a few days ago, I put on the shirt and went to meet my mother.

I thank you for the pictures. You look optimistic and kindhearted. You said that you had good friends and a nice family. It may be true that they are nice but I think you have the ability to be on intimate terms with people surrounding you.

There is a little possibility that the censor of this prison will not deliver a foreign letter to me, when a foreigner sends me a letter. But all the packages are delivered to me without exception. So I hope you to send me a letter with a package for the time being. How about sending me a package of a very small amount of chocolate which contains your letter? Even though you send me only a very small amount of chocolate and a letter, it's absolutely O.K. Do you know Malcolm Purves? Would you please inform Malcolm Purves, Roland Ginter, Isabelle Vonhoff and other friends of my new address and send them my best regards?

Yours sincerely,
Kim Seong-Man

The times are a-changin'. KSM is asked to work on the presidential campaign of Kim Dae Jung—from prison. In this letter, he also notes that the governor of the prison apologized to him for prior bad treatment. KSM also mentions being allowed to visit to an auto manufacturing plant.

97.9.11

Dear Drake Zimmerman,

Fall has come. Muggy weather has disappeared. We prisoners will have the best days in the year till it gets cold. I have recovered my health and am in good condition. I take breathing exercise everyday in my single room as soon as I get up. It lets me have a fresh mind and invigorates me.

I really want to thank you for your kindness and warm concern. The unused cards are very precious and I will use them, when I write to my friends. I was very pleased to receive so many unused cards. Soap and chocolate are of much value here. But the guard didn't hand over powdered chocolate to me. He told me that it was because he couldn't see if it contained a drug or not. I ask you not to send me powdered chocolate. I can't receive it in Taejeon prison.

I have been very busy in these days. A statesman, my senior, who belongs to an opposition party asked me to send her my idea of the strategy of the presidential election which will be in December. I have been very busy for weeks preparing for the report to send to my senior.

The candidate of the government party for the presidency in Korea is now very unpopular. He is the third among five candidates in surveys of public opinion. The candidate of the biggest opposition party is always the first in surveys. This is the fourth time for him to challenge the presidency. But he has high possibility to be elected this time. I hope him to be elected to the president. He did not spare any efforts for me to be granted commutation to life imprisonment nine years ago.

Now I live in a structure with foreign prisoners. There are about thirty foreign prisoners and I am the only Korean prisoner. Their crimes are mostly dope peddling and theft. Most of them are Asian and African people. There is an American. He was a swimming lecturer in Korea and is said to have had sex with a Korean lady by compulsion. Most foreign prisoners are very kind. We take exercise for an hour a day. I play basketball with foreigners every day. The American is the best player.

There are only a few foreigners who can speak English fluently in our structure. Prisoners manage to make themselves understood with English words, Korean words and gestures. Foreign prisoners like me very much. I help them not to be treated unreasonably by the guards. After I moved to this prison, I was also treated unreasonably for two months. The governor of the prison apologized to me for it. The governor and other guards now have a friendly way of dealing with me. I get along with them.

A few days ago I visited an auto factory outside the prison. The company has the objective to produce 2.5 million cars per year and to be the 10th biggest auto company in the world in the year 2000. I watched the assembling process with interest.

Yours sincerely,
Kim Seong Man

97.9.30

Dear Marie Anne De Rue,

I received your letter, picture and package with pleasure. The things in the package were very valuable here. I and my friends took them with relish. I am deeply grateful to you.

My parents live in Seoul, the capital city. My father is 76 years old and my mother is 71 years old. When they were young, cars were not popular in Korea. They don't know how to drive. They come here to visit me by a car which my brother or my sisters drive.

I have an older brother and two younger sisters. My brother is a company employee. One sister is a professor at a university which is the best in Korea, and the other sister is a teacher in a middle school. My family visits me one or two times a month, and my acquaintances sometimes visit me. But according to the rule of the prison, I can meet visitors only three times for a month.

There is no particular reason for me to be transferred to the new prison. Since I was imprisoned, I have been generally transferred to a new prison after about a year and a half. I have passed through seven prisons. This is the second time for me to live here, in Taejeon prison. Transfer is a good chance for me to have new experiences and to make friends with new persons. My thirties are filled with various experience in many prisons. The experience matured my personality.

I hope you to be in peace and happiness.

Yours sincerely,
Kim Seong Man

97.10.25

Dear Drake Zimmerman,

Nowadays the sky is blue, and the trees turn red and yellow.

I am on the second floor of a three-storied structure. The structure is located in the end of the prison, and I can see right outside the prison through the window in my room. I can see a mountain in a long distance, small hillocks in a short distance, a rice paddy field and several farmhouses over the high wall of the prison. When I get up early in the morning and remove windows from the window frame in my room to take breathing exercises I can see the animated and vivid sight of daybreak, and smell fresh air. In that case I am possessed with the illusion that I lead a rural life. But the sight is cracked vertically. It is cracked by lots of iron bars. So it sometimes looks like a folding screen.

Many persons go into the farmhouses and out of them frequently. They are men, aunts, grandfathers, grandmothers, and children. It is only novel in the prison to be able to see people outside the prison. It is more interesting for me to see persons walking than to see the fine view. If a sparrow sits on the top of the high wall of the prison, an adult outside the prison looks as big as the sparrow and a child looks as big by half of it. I can hear children chatter, but I can make nothing of what they say.

You asked me if it would be O.K. for you to share my letters with others. It's of course, O.K. But when I write send a few letters to a foreign country in the same period, the contents of a letter can be partly repeated. So there is a possibility that one may read partly repeated contents. I hope he will not regret it.

I want to enlarge men and women who are the size of a sparrow and their children who are the half size of a sparrow. Would you please send me a very small telescope which is the same as what you went me before? And I need colour pens, too. Would you please put a telescope and colour pens into the same package, it will be much easier for me to receive both of them from the guard who delivers packages to prisoners.

I hope you to be happy and in good health under the blue sky of fall.

Yours sincerely,
Kim Seong Man

1997.11.26

Dear Drake Zimmerman,

Winter has come. It is cold. The mountain and the rice paddy field outside the prison look a little desolate. People who go in and come out the farmhouses incessantly diminished apparently. Men and women who are as big as a sparrow wear thick clothes all together and I can't tell with ease whether one is male or a female.

I am in good health. The floor of my room is ice-cold. If I sit on a cushion on the floor for 20 minutes, moisture comes into being between the cushion and the floor because of the gap of the temperature of my body and the floor. I spend the day, sitting on a chair. I warm my feet, wearing three socks at the same time in my room.

My family visits me one or two times for a month, and my friends often visit me. There are double panes of glass between visitors and me in a meeting room, and there are many iron bars between the panes of glass. The panes have many small holes that visitors and I may hear each other. The holes are so small that I can't take their hands or fingers. One special chance is given to me for a month or two months that I can meet my family in a room which has no panes and iron bars but a table and a sofa. I can talk with my family in the room in comfort for thirty minutes.

We will have a presidential election on December 18, in this year. The leader of an opposition party, Kim Dae-Jung, still ranks first in a survey of public opinion. He has high possibility to be elected, but he can be defeated. A new president will be inaugurated on February 25, next year. Whoever is elected, the new president will grant amnesty to prisoners of conscience of the day of inauguration. Amnesty on the day is thought to be a golden opportunity for me to be released. Many people have made an effort for my release and now expect that I will be free on the day. If senators and congressmen in USA sign a petition for my release and send it to a successful candidate in January next year, it will exert a great influence on my amnesty. I sent a letter to Dr. Jae Hyun Lee a few days ago and asked him to get a petition of senators and congressmen and to send it to a successful candidate. In 1989 he got a petition and sent it to the president of Korea. I asked him to make an effort again. A new petition will have a powerful influence this time. Would you please call Dr. Jae Hyun Lee and discuss the petition? I want your help.

Yours sincerely,
Kim Seong Man

GROUP CORRESPONDENCE

Clare McVey's Group Correspondence message dated December 16, 1997 reflected our collective optimism that Kim Song-man would be released after the Korean Presidential election scheduled for later in the week.

The Korean political custom of granting amnesty to prisoners in honor of a presidential inauguration loomed hopefully on the horizon. It all depended, of course, upon which candidate prevailed in the election.

Clare also informed us that KSM's case was to be featured "as a Worldwide Appeal" in the February edition of AI's international newsletter.

"This will give us an opportunity to lobby the new President for Kim Song-man's release during the month of February," she noted.

Dear Drake Zimmerman,
1997. 12. 14.

We had a heavy snow a few days ago. A mountain, a rice paddy field and farmhouses which I can see in my room are covered with snow. The world is pure white.

Korea is now in an economic crisis. All the people are embarrassed very much.

A new president will be elected a few days later. I hope he will reconstruct my country's economy. And I expect that he will pay regard to human rights and release me and other prisoners of conscience.

I am deeply grateful to you for your warm heart. I sent you a letter on November 26. I hope you received it.

I hope you will have a merry Christmas season. I wish you and Jan good luck and good health in the coming year.

Yours sincerely,

새 해 복 많이 받으십시오.
(= Happy New Year!)

KSM explains his link with Korea's newly-elected president. Before the election, Kim Dae-Jung was a member of the National Assembly, and he led the effort to have Kim Song-man's sentence commuted to life imprisonment. Kim Dae-Jung had a parallel fate to KSM, in that he had also been imprisoned on political charges, was sentenced to death, then had his sentence commuted. He was later released.

1998.1.8

Dear Susan M. Clary,

I have a schedule to watch TV in this afternoon. I am able to watch TV once a week. I mainly choose entertainment programs. Before imprisonment I didn't watch TV except news programs. But it is very amusing to watch entertainment programs in jail. Maybe it's because the prison life is monotonous and boring. And there is one more reason: I can find ladies only in TV. To observe and find female entertainers' character and personality is very interesting.

Ten days ago there was execution in Korea. Twenty-three prisoners under death sentence were put to death in four prisons at the same time. Six prisoners were put to death in this prison. On the day of execution there was no exercise time, and it was silent as a graveyard at midnight. The president-elect who was elected last month is a statesman who has insisted on the abolition of capital punishment. He will be inaugurated next month. It is not certain if he will abolish capital punishment, but with hope are we able to expect that he will commute the sentence of death of some prisoners. The present government executed a death sentence only two months before the inauguration of a new president. I don't like this government. According to a survey of public opinion the present president is supported by less than 10% of the people.

Korea had a misfortune and a fortune last month. The misfortune was that Korea's economy was nearly bankrupt and was supported by IMF. The fortune was that the leader of an opposition party who had belief in democracy was elected to the president. He is also a man who saved my life nine years ago. When I was a prisoner under sentence of death, he, a leader of an opposition party, negotiated with the government and drew my commutation from death sentence to life imprisonment in 1988. He will be inaugurated in February 25. He will grant amnesty to some prisoners of conscience on inauguration. I hope to be free on the day.

Yours sincerely,
Kim Seong Man

1998.1.19

Dear Drake Zimmerman,

I received your card with pleasure. I deeply thank you for your favor to visit me after my release. I also would like to meet you and Jan very much.

Dr. Lee Jae Hyun is a professor of Western Illinois University. His major is journalism. In the letter which he sent me a few years ago, he told me that it was desirable for me to keep on corresponding with you. So I guessed that you knew him or you had met him in A.I. meeting a few times. I am sorry that I requested you to contact him whom you didn't know.

The president-elect in Korea plans to grant clemency to some prisoners of conscience soon after his inauguration. It is not certain yet that I will be included. Domestic organizations for human rights ask him to release all the prisoners of conscience. Besides a few acquaintances of the president-elect individually ask him to set me free.

One million people will be dismissed in Korea in this year, and many people will have their wage cut down. All the Koreans are unhappy now. Prices are rising rapidly already, and the quality of side dishes in jail will be fallen soon.

We had snow almost every day in these days. Now it is snowing hard and fast outside. It snows almost every day on the white world covered with snow. A snowslide deprived 6 college students of their lives a few days ago. They were climbing a mountain. Exercise hours are given to prisoners on snowy days, too. But we can't play basketball or soccer because the land is covered with snow. I can't play a game. But I am in good health.

Yours sincerely,
Kim Seong Man

Part Six

Yearning: The Last Days in Prison

"…the latest information we have about Kim Song-man is that his sentence has been reduced to 20 years' imprisonment. We are still awaiting confirmation of the details of all the reductions in sentence, so if there is any change in the news about Kim Song-man we'll pass it on to you."

From a letter to USA AI Group 202 written by Sylvia Lindsay of the East Asia Team dated 18 March 1998

1998.3.17

Dear Drake Zimmerman,

It is the time of dawning. I am writing you a letter, still being in my single room in Taejeon Prison. A small noise made by running cars in the long distance reaches my ear.

With great pleasure did I receive Viktor Frankl's book, underwear, gloves, a cap and so on. I wanted to talk to you over the phone after my release rather than to send you a letter. But the particular pardon carried out in memory of the new president's inauguration didn't set me free, and I am still in Taejeon Prison. But my life imprisonment was commuted to twenty years. The new president's party has less than one-third of seats in the National Assembly. On the other hand, the biggest opposition party has the majority of seats. The opposition party is very conservative and has a dislike for the president's program of rapid reform. The party has a positive objection to release of prisoners of conscience. The prisoners of conscience who were set free by the particular pardon were mostly college students and laborers and the prisoners who were over seventy years old. The president is going to grant clemency to prisoners of conscience once more in this year after he consolidates his political power.

I go to bed early and get up early at dawn. I began my work again to obtain knowledge from books in my single room. And I read books for a few hours at dawn. Now I have been reading the Norton Anthology of World Masterpieces. To read a book is certainly amusing and always gives me pleasure.

I heard that lots of letters from U.S.A. and other countries had reached the president. I guess that you gave me a helping hand and put forth efforts. I am deeply grateful to you.

Clare McVey in U.K. made a beneficial effort and sent my mother a letter of consolation and encouragement. And I heard that my friends in Belgium also helped me. I am thankful to Clare McVey and friends in Belgium.

Missing the day when I will talk to you on the phone in my house.

Yours sincerely,
Kim Seong-man

1998.5.17

Dear Drake Zimmerman,

U.S.A. is heard to have been under prosperous economic conditions for 7 years. I guess your business goes very well too. I hope your business prospers and you save much money in these good times.

I am in good health. I observe Korean political activity attentively. My release is thought to depend upon it. The power of the new president who has will to set me free and has belief in democracy and social reform is still weak. We will have an election for local self-governments on June 4. If the ruling party wins a political victory in the election, the president will get stronger political power. He has a plan to release prisoners of conscience on August 15, which is an anniversary of the liberation from Japanese Imperialists. I hope the president will have stronger power till that day.

I have been reading a book, 'How to Be Rich' written by J. Paul Getty. His book and his life are very interesting. I was not born of a very rich family, nor born of a poor family. I have not suffered from economic distress till now. So I have had, I think, no chance to develop a good principle of my own on money. Reading the book, I have realized that I had an immature idea of the way not only how to earn money but how to use money. The book taught me a useful lesson.

Early summer is just ahead. The scenery which I can see in my room is beautiful. Few people walked along a road in winter, but now men and women pass by very often. We can sometimes find ladies on the road. Prisoners shout and call the ladies or give them a big whistle. But there are no ladies who turn around and show an interest. Generally speaking, prisoners are isolated from society by a high wall, and prisoners can hardly see people outside the prison and, especially, ladies.

How is Jan Elfline? I hope she is in good health and happiness.

Yours sincerely,
Kim Seong Man

KSM looks forward to a "socially valuable life." His sister lived in Normal, Illinois (where I also lived at the time) for a semester while completing her doctorate. A friend of mine, I discovered, was in the same doctoral program with KSM's sister. Somehow, the world became just a bit smaller with a casual conversation beginning with, "The brother of a close friend of mine is in prison in Korea..."!

1998.7.22

Dear Drake Zimmerman,

I received your card of July 6 with gratitude. I am deeply grateful to you for your constant and heartful concern.

It is within the realms of high possibility for me to be released in the pardon in memory of Independence Day. The president and the government have will to release prisoners of conscience on August 15 and in case of me they have strong will. The government is said to have a plan to release prisoners of conscience, including me, at 10 a.m. on August 14. (August 15 is a holiday and prisoners are generally set free on the day before a holiday.)

When I am set free, I will go to Seoul where my house and my parents are. I will telephone you within a few days in Seoul. I can read and write English of course. But I feel a little difficulty in speaking and listening, for I have had little chance to speak English in the prison for 13 years. When I talk with you over the telephone in English, my younger sister who got a doctor's degree in the University of Chicago will help me. I think I need a few months' practice after my release to speak English fluently.

Will you please send my best regards to Jan Elfline and to Bob Connelly? I am very sorry that I have not sent a letter to Bob Connelly for a long time. But I thank him for his friendship and kindness.

I think it is very hot now in Normal.

Yours sincerely,
Kim Seong-man

8 August 98

Dear Friends of Kim Song-man and Amnesty International Group #202,

This is not a done deal, but it looks very likely that our Group #202 Prisoner of Conscience for the last 10 years, South Korean dissident Kim Song-man, is due to be released this Thursday. If he is part of the large general release, with the time difference, his release would come for us about 9 p.m. on the 13th. Yes, this Thursday.

I have invited him to visit Bloomington-Normal. If you want to meet him, let me know, provided he accepts the invitation and is able to come. We would take him to Western Illinois University to visit and let him do whatever he wants.

Watch the news for KSM's release!

Thank you so much for writing the letters and sending the packages over the last 10+ years.

Excerpt from a memo to AI Group #202
From Drake Zimmerman

Epilogue

Free at Last

Kim Seong-man walks out of Taejeon Prison
accompanied by his mother, Choi In-hwa.

(Photographs in this section are courtesy of Kim Song-man.)

Kim Seong-man speaks to the media in front of Taejeon Prison.

Pierre Sane, left, secretary general of Amnesty
International and Kim Seong-man.

1998.10.7

Dear Drake Zimmerman,

I have been very busy after release. I have met many people and expressed my thanks to all who helped me while I was in jail, and meetings with celebrities including members of the National Assembly are continued.

My mother is now in great happiness to be with her second son, me, after the lapse of 13 years and 2 months. I am happy day by day, too. I felt happiness when I watched a big baseball game in the stadium or when I bit a 'Big Mac' in a McDonald's and felt the taste for the first time in 13 years. (I was desirous to eat a 'Big Mac' for thirteen years.)

Only a man who is alive can see the blue sky and feel the joy of life. Realizing the real valuableness of life and freedom, I get along.

I am deeply grateful to you and Jan Elfline from the bottom of my heart for your efforts to release me and your consolation of letters and packages.

I hope you will have a happy birthday. I hope the new year will be a pleasant one when you will achieve what you want to, and you will be in good health and in happiness. Happy birthday to you.

I have not sent letters to friends in foreign countries, yet. Would you please send my best regards to Bob Connelly, Susan M. Clary and other friends in America?

Yours sincerely,
Kim Seong-man

March 1, 1999

Dear Drake Zimmerman:

I am very sorry to send you a reply letter very late. I always feel grateful to you, Jan Elfline and other friends in U.S.A. for having helped and encouraged me when I was in the prison. I am hopeful that our warm friendship will be eternal.

After my release I could hardly feel that it was a reality for a few months. I had dreamt a free life for more than 13 years, and it was my desperate hope when I was under the sentence of death. I think it's a rule that when one achieves what he has dreamt for a long time, he can't tell if it is a dream or a reality. Now 6 months after my release, I almost recovered the sense of reality.

For a few months after my release I had the same emotion that I had in the prison. It really brought me an uneasiness to walk on the street by myself unrestrictedly. I have never walked by myself without a guard for 13 years.

Now I remember the uneasiness and fear which I felt when I was in a narrow elevator with a lady. A man's prison is the area forbidden to women. But prisoners sometimes come across the female staff in an office. In such a case prisoners must not approach or talk to her. They are roundly scolded if they look up into her face for a while. When I was with the lady in a narrow elevator, I really felt uneasy and fearful, for I had the same emotion that I had in the prison. But 6 months have passed since I was released, and now maybe the lady would be uneasy in that case.

Now I live in my house where I had lived 13 years ago. I wear the same clothes that I wore before. It looks like a miracle to me when I recall the despair under the sentence of death. I feel a great joy in the miracle.

I came back to the environment familiar to me. I resumed my social life which had been cut off. I feel as if I had traveled for a week. How long will the period of 13 years be which look like a week to me? My nephew gives me the answer. My nephew who was not born when I was first imprisoned is now in the first grade in a middle school, and there are his books wholly on his bookshelves. Looking at him, I realize how long I lived in the prison.

I have been busy as a bee since I was released. I had to meet many people and was invited to many places. I could hardly read a newspaper, and came to know that my news was printed in newspapers or magazines, being told the fact by others.

I am going to make an effort for human rights and the reunification of Korea. I am in a good health. I was put to a very thorough medical examinations after my release and I was told that I had no disease. I am really grateful to you and American friends who prayed for my health. You and Jan Elfline, Bob Connelly and his wife, Jan, Susan M. Clary, and other American friends are really my good friends whom I can't forget forever.

Yours sincerely,
Kim Seong-man

Kim Seong-man, second from left, at an outdoor rally 11-25-99.

12/9/99

Dear Drake Zimmerman,

When I was a prisoner under the sentence of death, I used to sit humming this hymn alone in my single room.

"Hail to the brightness of Zion's glad morning.
Joy to the lands that in darkness have dawn.
Hushed to sorrow and mourning ;
Zion in triumph begins her mild reign."

The purpose of the hymn was to taste an ultimate exultation I would have felt if the death sentence could be finally commuted. Chances were, however, very thin that it could happen. It seemed almost impossible for me to survive at that time. Now, whenever I drink a cup of coffee in some nice place, looking back on those days when I hummed a hymn, it looks like a miracle for me to live a free life in society.

When I look back at my past life as a condemned prisoner, I find a life with a deep sorrow. It was destined to be ended sooner or later. The most painful was to realize that I couldn't do anything more which I wanted to do and I couldn't actualize my dream in my life.

Well, here I am, feeling my heart beating and I enjoy my free life. What do I want to do and what is my dream now? I had two alternatives in my mind when I was released in August last year. I decided to choose one of them after experiencing a social life for one year or so. One choice was to participate in international human rights movement and the other was to strive for reunification of Korean peninsula. A test period of about 15 months has made me decide to concentrate on the latter while setting the former as a long-term goal.

I am giving lectures in universities, churches, and civil NGOs [nongovernmental organizations, i.e. CARE, Rotary, Catholic Social Services]. The lecture covers topics from human rights improvement in Korea, the abolishment of The National Security Law, to the reconciliation of the conservatives and the progressives in Korea. Besides making public addresses, I sometimes meet people from both sides, the conservatives and the progressives, in order to know how they stand apart from each other in terms of the reunification. Now I attend Yonsei Graduate School specializing in the reunification of Korean peninsula. I would like to make an important contribution to make the two separated Koreas come closer and eventually become one. I will send you a picture by airmail. You will notice that I and participants of the outdoor gathering are singing a song to urge the government to taking roots of all sorts of tortures.

More than one year of a social life outside of prison has changed me into a refined gentleman. I returned my hair, which had disappeared during the period under the death sentence to the original state by the power of a wig. I look in my 30s after wearing a wig without which I looked in my 50s because of a baldhead. Even ladies in their 20s show me kindness now.

One of the frequently asked questions is what is the most difficult thing to deal with after going through such a long isolated period. To tell the truth, I have had a trouble in getting along with ladies. I guess it's not so difficult to imagine how hard it would be for me to regard a woman in her 40s as my partner considering I was imprisoned at age of 28 and had few chances to talk to woman in prison for a long period. I have found myself to feel more comfortable with ladies in their 20s or in the early part of 30s. Ladies over the age look to me older than I. I feel comfortable with a young lady. The problem is that when I talk with a young lady frankly, she tends to feel burdened for my unreserved emotion. To adjust myself to my age is one of the hardest things.

Before imprisonment I took only one thing as the most valuable pleasure to pursue while disregarding other aspects of pleasure. It was 'a spiritual pleasure.' By pursuit of 'a socially valuable life' my life could be meaningful. And living up to the rule certainly gave me the peace of mind breaking the wall between life and death. Since I set the rule for my life, I have never had a doubt in my mind over the importance of 'a socially valuable life' and it even got stronger while I was in prison. I could realize that the rule was more valuable to me than my life when I was a prisoner under the sentence of death. However during the long period of imprisonment I came to realize that 'a spiritual pleasure ' might not be the only one I should pursue. 'An emotional pleasure' was also important.

Living a life for more than 13 years where 'an emotional pleasure' was almost forfeited, I could realize that gifts from God were not only 'a spiritual pleasure' but also 'an emotional pleasure.' After being released, I sometimes go to the movies and learn how to sing various songs from a teacher. I feel happy being engaged in a joyful conversation which is intelligent and humorous with my acquaintances in a coffee shop. I am alive and free. I enjoy not only a spiritual pleasure and an emotional pleasure. It's like having some kind of a small party when I have a happy day.

It will be a great pleasure for me if you can stop by Seoul during your journey in January. Please certainly let me know if you are going to visit Seoul. And I'd like to have a chance to visit U. S. A. to meet several good friends including you, Jan Elfline, Bob Connelly, Steven F. Monk, and David W. Babson and visit offices of International Amnesty bodies there. I guess the good timing for my U.S. visit will be when you publish the book which is a collection of my letters. I will do my best to visit U. S. A. I think there is high possibility for me to visit U. S. A. if you help me, by sending someone's invitation document to me for example.

I say that it is at your disposal to choose the letters to be included in the book. You can choose anything from what you have including the suicide note. The last Christmas in the 1900s is just three weeks away. I wish you will have a New Year that is full of vision, hope and happiness.

Merry Christmas!
Kim Song-Man

HAIL TO THE BRIGHTNESS OF ZION'S GLAD MORNING!
Words: Thomas Hastings,
Spiritual Songs for Social Worship, 1831
Music: "Wesley (Mason)," Lowell Mason, 1830

Hail to the brightness of Zion's glad morning!
Joy to the lands that in darkness have lain!
Hushed be the accents of sorrow and mourning;
Zion in triumph begins her mild reign.

Hail to the brightness of Zion's glad morning!
Long by the prophets of Israel foretold!
Hail to the millions from bondage returning!
Gentiles and Jews the blest vision behold.

Lo, in the desert rich flowers are springing,
Streams ever copious are gliding along;
Loud from the mountain tops echoes are ringing,
Wastes rise in verdure, and mingle in song.

See, from all lands, from the isles of the ocean,
Praise to the Savior ascending on high;
Fallen the engines of war and commotion;
Shouts of salvation are rending the sky.

August 15, 2000

Today is the second anniversary of Kim Song-man's release. Today South Korean President Kim Dae-jung announced an additional amnesty for over 30,000 offenses ranging from parking violations to low-level corruption. In addition, he said he planned to revise the National Security Law, long criticized by the United States and human rights groups. It was this National Security Law that was used to imprison Kim Song-man and many others who advocated the reunification of the two Koreas.

Today, too, 100 families from North and South Korea are reuniting for the first time in decades. The recent summit meeting of leaders from North and South Korea points toward a melting of hostilities between the Koreas and provides hope of eventual reunification. A dark era appears to be coming to an end. In thinking of this new day, we picture Kim Song-man's smiling face and hold his spirit of hope as inspiration in our hearts.

Thank you, Song Man, for sharing your spirit with us all!

Drake Zimmerman CFA JD
P.O. Box 326
Normal, IL 61761 309-454-7040
FAX: 309-454-6914 drake.zimmerman@gte.net

Drake Zimmerman is an investment advisor based in Normal, Illinois. From 1985-1998 Drake served as group leader for Amnesty International Adoption Group #202 of Normal, Illinois and as the U.S. case coordinator for Kim Song-man's case. A past president of his Rotary Club, he founded Rotarians Against Malaria and co-founded the Community Foundation of McLean County. He lives in the country with his wife Jan Elfline and keeps bees.

Appendix

새해에는 더욱 건강하시고
뜻하시는 일 모두 이루시기 바랍니다.

Dear Drake Zimmerman

I wish you many happy returns
of the day.

Amnesty International

INTERNATIONAL SECRETARIAT
1 Easton Street London WC1X 8DJ
United Kingdom

RECOMMENDED CASE ACTION

The instructions below are to guide your action on this particular case. If nothing is said to the contrary, you may, after studying these instructions, undertake additional actions suggested in the enclosed General Instructions booklet.

DATE: 21 August 1989
PRISONER: Kim Song-man
COUNTRY: South Korea

Before you begin work on this case, please refer to the chapter on casework in the latest edition of the AI Handbook.

You will read, in the background to the "1985 Western Illinois Campus Spy Ring" case, that 20 people were arrested in September 1985 on charges of espionage for North Korea. At the time of the arrests there was little information on the exact charges against the prisoners and of the activities that led to their arrest. The Research Department has, since September 1985, obtained further documents and met with sources in Korea who provided sufficient information to confirm that two of the six prisoners still detained in this case are prisoners of conscience and should be adopted by AI groups. There is now also evidence that the remaining four prisoners may also be prisoners of conscience and their cases are being allocated to groups for further investigation. The prisoners of conscience in this case have been allocated to three groups each, the investigation cases to two groups each.

The emphasis of work for the groups who have been allocated the cases of prisoners of conscience, Kim Song-man and Hwang Tae-kwon, is to appeal to the South Korean authorities for their immediate and unconditional release and to publicize their cases and gather appeals on their behalf in their own countries. Those groups working for the prisoners under investigation, Yang Dong-hwa, Kang Yong-ju, Chong Kum-taek and Kim Chang-kyu, are asked to seek further details of the charges against the prisoners and the evidence used to convict them from the authorities as well as from non-government sources in South Korea and abroad. All groups should raise AI's concerns about allegations that some or all of the prisoners were subjected to torture and ill-treatment to force them to confess to the charges against them. Contact with the families of the prisoners, where possible, is encouraged.

1. When you receive the case sheet

Please read the case sheet and all background material carefully before starting work. If you have difficulty in translating or understanding any of the information, ask for guidance from your Coordination group or section.

2. Writing letters to government authorities

2.1 Please write courteously worded and polite letters, typed if possible, to the government officials on the Government Authorities List. The South Korean authorities rarely reply to letters, but this does not mean that they do not read them and this should not discourage you from writing regularly.

2.2 The most important government officials to whom you should write appealing for your prisoner's release are: the President, Minister of Justice, Prime Minister, Foreign Minister and Minister of Home Affairs.

2.3 Your letters should be written in your own language or English. Letters may be written in Korean only if you are completely confident that the translation is perfect.

2.4 Please write your first letter to all government officials on AI-headed note paper, and about half your letters thereafter. In letters on AI-headed correspondence, you should introduce yourselves as an AI group, giving a brief description of the concerns of AI according to the Statute. You should emphasize particularly the independent nature of AI by, for example, mentioning prisoners or campaigns in other parts of the world for whom your group is working.
Alternatively, in some of your letters you may enclose a copy of the "AI Objectives" leaflet in Korean. Five copies of this leaflet are enclosed with your casesheet.

2.5 The other letters to government authorities from your group should be written from a private address or, when possible, in a professional capacity.

2.6 Please remember there is no standard way of transliterating Korean into roman script, so the identity of the prisoner about whom you are writing may not be immediately apparent to the recipient of your letter. It is therefore important that you give full details about your prisoner: name, date of arrest, legislation under which he is held, prison and prisoner number, if these are known. The Korean characters for prisoners' names are given whenever possible. If these are provided for your prisoner, you may carefully copy the simple phonetic Korean characters onto letters you send to Korea.

2.7 Letters should express concern that Kim Song-man is detained for visiting North Korea and that he is held for the peaceful expression of his political opinions. Urge that immediate consideration be given to his case and that he be granted a prompt and unconditional release.

2.8 You should also express concern that Kim Song-man referred to having been ill-treated during this interrogation. Ask that an investigation be immediately initiated into these allegations, and that any official found guilty of carrying out such ill-treatment be punished according to the law.

2.9 International human rights guarantees and articles in South Korean laws that may be used when writing to the South Korean authorities:

Detention for peaceful political activities and expression of opinion

Universal Declaration of Human Rights: "Everyone has the right to freedom of opinion and expression; this right includes freedom to hold opinions without interference and to seek, receive and impart information and ideas through any media and regardless of frontiers."
Article 21 of the Constitution of the Republic of Korea: "All citizens shall enjoy freedom of speech and the press, and freedom of assembly and association."

On the prohibition of torture and ill-treatment

Universal Declaration of Human Rights—Article 5: "No one shall be subjected to torture or to cruel, inhuman or degrading treatment."

International Covenant on Economic, Social and Cultural rights—Article 7: as above.

Article 12 (2) of the Constitution of the Republic of Korea: "No citizen shall be tortured or compelled to testify against himself in criminal cases."

Article 12(7) of the Constitution of the Republic of Korea: "In a case where a confession is deemed to have been made against a defendant's will by means of torture, violence, intimidation, unduly prolonged arrest, deceit, etc., or in a case where a confession is the only evidence against a defendant in a formal trial, such a confession shall not be admitted as evidence of guilt nor shall a defendant be punished by reason of such a confession."

Right to be informed of reason for arrest

International Covenant on Civil and Political Rights— Article 9.2: "Anyone who is arrested shall be informed, at the time of arrest, of the reasons for his arrest and shall be promptly informed of any charges against him."

Article 12(5) of the Constitution of the Republic of Korea: "No person shall be arrested or detained without being informed of the reason therefore and of his right to assistance of counsel. The family, etc., as designated by law, of a person arrested or detained shall be notified without delay of the reason for and the time and place of the arrest or detention."

On habeas corpus

International Covenant on Civil and Political Rights—Article 9.4: "Anyone who is deprived of his liberty by arrest or detention shall be entitled to take proceedings before a court, in order that that court may decide without delay on the lawfulness of his detention and order his release if the detention is not lawful."

Constitution of the Republic of Korea—Article 12(6): "Any person who is arrested or detained shall have the right to request the court to review the legality of the arrest or detention."

<u>On compensation</u>

International Covenant on Civil and Political Rights—Article 9.5: "Anyone who has been the victim of unlawful arrest or detention shall have an enforceable right to compensation."

You can quote from the Universal Declaration of Human Rights (adopted by the United Nations) which says:

Article 19: "Everyone has the right to freedom of opinion and expression; this right includes freedom to hold opinions without interference and to seek, receive and impart information and ideas through any media and regardless of frontiers."

Please send copies of your letters to the embassy of the Republic of Korea in your country.

2.10 Letters may also be written to the Human Rights Committee of the opposition parties, as well as of the ruling Democratic Justice Party, introducing yourselves as AI members working on Kim Song-man's behalf and urging that they appeal to the appropriate authorities for his release. See the government authorities list for addresses.

2.11 Please do not confuse the government of South Korea with that of the Democratic People's Republic of Korea (North Korea) who should never be approached on matters concerning South Korea.

3. Collecting information from other sources

3.1
> IMPORTANT! PLEASE READ CAREFULLY!
>
> Families and all associates of political prisoners in South Korea are in a most precarious position. Their mail may be scrutinized by the authorities. Families, friends and lawyers of political prisoners may be detained, put under house arrest or surveillance by the National Agency for Security Planning (formerly known as the Korean Central Intelligence Agency) or other security forces. Article 104(2) of the Criminal Code provides a maximum of seven years imprisonment for "slandering or defaming the Republic of Korea or its state organizations from abroad or at home with the help of foreigners or foreign organizations."
>
> Please do not write to any addresses in the Republic of Korea not mentioned in these Recommended Actions without first consulting the Asia Research Department.

3.2 The Korean Federal Bar Association is active in human rights issues in South Korea and has openly expressed its concerns about detention of political prisoners and torture to the government. Letters can be written in either a private or personal capacity requesting that they send appeals for Kim Song-man's release to the appropriate authorities.

Human Rights Committee
Korean Federal Bar Association
160 Tangju-dong
Chongno-gu
Seoul

3.3 Similar letters to the above can be sent to:

International Human Rights League of Korea
340-2, 2-ga, Taepyong-ro
Chung-gu
Seoul

3.4 Approaches to Local Human Rights Groups: for guidelines on approaches to local human rights groups, please see circular ASA 25/22/88 included in the prisoner dossier.

3.5 While on a research mission to South Korea in July 1988, AI delegates interviewed Kim Song-man's family, which is actively campaigning for his release. You may wish to write to Kim Song-man's sister, who lives in Chicago, explaining that you are the group in your country working for Kim Song-man's release. Welcome any news she may have about her brother and ask if she could send your best wishes to her family. You may also try to contact the family through Minkahyop, whose address is given in the enclosed circular, on approaches to human rights groups. The family does not speak English and are unlikely to be able to reply to your letters, but will gain comfort and encouragement from them.

Ms Kim Hye-lan
5751 South Woodlawn Avenue, Apt. 5/15
Chicago
Illinois 60637
USA

3.6   You may also write to Western Illinois University, where some students and staff have made appeals on behalf of Kim Song-man and Yang Dong-hwa. Explain that you are an AI group working for the release of Kim Song-man and would like to contact students and staff members who knew him when he was a student at the university. Ask if the university administration would be so kind as to forward you letter to the appropriate persons.

Western Illinois University
Macomb
Illinois 61455
USA

4. Letters to the Prison

Kim Song-man is detained in Taejon Prison. Letters should be addressed as follows:

Kim Song-man
Taejon Prison
I Choongchon-dong
Choongnam 300
Republic of Korea

4.1   Letters and parcels are sometimes passed on to prisoners or are given to them upon their release.

4.2   Your letter should be short (a greeting card is ideal) and contain a message of friendly greetings. It is best not to mention AI by name, and you must not mention the political situation in South Korea.

4.3   Send your letter to the Prison Director with a short polite covering note asking him to pass the letter to your prisoner. Again, do not mention AI or the political situation in South Korea.

4.4   If the letter to your prisoner is returned from South Korea, please write immediately to the Korean National Red Cross to ask for information about his current place of detention. The letter should be written on plain notepaper from a private address. Please do not mention AI in the letter, and do not include any appeals for your prisoner's release, etc. The address is:

Korean National Red Cross
32, 3-ga Namsan-dong
Chung-gu
Seoul
Republic of Korea

5. Appeals from target sectors in your own country

5.1   You may wish to ask members of your own government to send appeals for Kim Song-man's release to the South Korean authorities. Please discuss this with your coordinator (or section office if there is no coordinator) before taking action.

5.2   Many countries have embassies in Korea, to which groups may wish to write requesting the ambassador for their country to send appeals for Kim Song-man's release. Please contact your South Korea coordinator for the address of the embassy. If there is no South Korea coordinator in your section, please write to the Asia Research Department at the International Secretariat for the address.

5.3   As Kim Song-man was a student of physics and political science, you may find that students in your country will be willing to also send appeals for his release. As Kim Song-man comes from a family that had founded the Evangelical Church in Korea, you may ask members of the Evangelical Churches in your local community to also make appeals for his release.

6. Replies

Please send copies of any replies concerning your prisoner to the International Secretariat as soon as possible.

7. Publicity

7.1   You may give publicity to this case following the recommendations given in the Handbook for Groups.

7.2   You may find it useful to organize publicity to coincide with South Korean national holidays. The main holidays are:

1 March	Independence Movement Day (declaration of independence made by 33 Koreans against Japanese rule on 1 March 1919)

19 April	Anniversary of the Student Uprising (on 19 April 1960, students rebelled against conduct of the presidential elections, in which then-President Syngman Rhee was reelected. The president resigned shortly afterwards.)
5 May	Children's Day (this was declared a holiday in 1975; its purpose is to allow parents and children to spend a day together.
May (Lunar 8 April)	Buddha's Birthday
17 July	Constitution Day (commemorates the founding of the Republic of Korea and the promulgation of the constitution in 1948)
15 August	National Liberation Day (marks the anniversary of the surrender of Japan in 1945 and the establishment of the Republic of Korea in 1948)
3 October	National Foundation Day (according to mythology, the national founder, Tangun, descended to earth on this day)
25 December	Christmas

7.3 Copies of any local or national news items on your groups' activities should be sent to the South Korean embassy in your country, and to the Ministry of Foreign Affairs in South Korea.

8. Note Re. Korean Names

The family name is always given before the given name. Therefore Kim Song-man is referred to as Mr. Kim. As there are relatively few family names in Korea, it always best to use the full name when writing to the country to avoid confusion. Whenever possible, the Korean characters for your prisoner's name are given on the casesheet.

Most Korean characters are simple to reproduce and you may wish to copy them carefully onto your letters to aid identification. (Korean women do not take on their husbands' family names when they get married, although the children do.)

<u>Attachments</u>

Government Authorities List	INTERNAL
South Korea: Human Rights Guarantees in New Constitution	EXTERNAL
South Korea: Detention of Prisoners of Conscience and Torture Continue	EXTERNAL
South Korea entry *Far Eastern Economic Yearbook 1989*	EXTERNAL
AI's Objectives in Korean x 5 (plus English translation)	EXTERNAL
Photograph of Kim Song-man	EXTERNAL

AMNESTY INTERNATIONAL

REPUBLIC OF KOREA (SOUTH KOREA):

CASE SUMMARY. KIM SONG-MAN

Name/date of birth:	KIM Song-man(m), born 10 October 1957
Occupation:	- Graduate of physics from Yonsei University, Seoul - Studied political science at Western Illinois University in the USA
Date and place of arrest:	6 June 1985, Seoul
Charge:	Charged under the National Security Law with "espionage" and "anti-state" activities for North Korea
Sentence:	- Sentenced to death by Seoul District Court on 20 January 1986 - Sentence upheld by Seoul High Court in May 1986 and by the Supreme Court in December 1986 - Commuted to life imprisonment in December 1988
Prison:	Currently held in Taejon Prison (but has been moved many times)
Family:	Mother lives in Seoul
Health:	Currently in good health
Related cases:	Three other prisoners still held in this case
Photo:	Old photo, taken before his arrest
AI Concern:	AI has adopted Kim Song-man as a prisoner of conscience and is calling for his immediate and unconditional release. AI believes he was convicted unfairly, on the basis of a confession extracted under torture.

POLITICAL AND LEGAL CONTEXT

There are over 50 long-term political prisoners in South Korea, half of whom are over the age of 60. They have all spent over seven years in prison, and some have been in prison for several decades. Sentenced to long prison terms for national security offences under past governments, they are South Korea's forgotten prisoners.

Amnesty International (AI) is campaigning on behalf of a smaller group of long-term political prisoners who were arrested during the 1970s and 1980s and sentenced to long prison terms after unfair trials. AI has documented 20 of these cases but believes there may be at least a dozen more.

These long-term political prisoners were convicted in the context of a divided Korea. Since the Korean War (1950-53) the governments of North Korea (the Democratic People's Republic of Korea) and South Korea (the Republic of Korea) have prohibited almost all contact between citizens of the two countries. In South Korea, unauthorized contacts have often resulted in imprisonment under the National Security Law.

These prisoners were arrested and tried under South Korea's National Security Law. Many were students and businessmen at the time of their arrest. Some had travelled abroad and had been in contact with North Koreans, some had lived in Japan or had relatives in Japan. They were accused of passing "state secrets" to North Korean agents in other countries and other espionage activities. In these cases there is evidence of illegal arrest, incommunicado detention for a long period of time, claims by the prisoners that they were forced to confess under torture and a lack of facilities in the preparation of a defense. Amnesty International believes they were convicted largely on the basis of confessions which were extracted under torture.

The prisoners were arrested and convicted at a time when human rights violations were widespread. During most of these two decades, the country was ruled by authoritarian military governments. General Park Chang-hee seized power in 1961 and held the office of president until his assassination in 1979. Another army general, Chun Doo-hwan, became president in 1980 and held office until 1987, when he was forced by popular protests to call a direct presidential election. He was succeeded by Roh Tae-woo, who held office until 1993.

The National Security Law has been amended very little over the decades. It provides long prison terms for unauthorized contacts with North Koreans, for "praising" and "benefitting" North Korea and forming or joining organizations alleged to be "anti-state" (or pro-North Korean). It also provides long sentences or the death penalty for "espionage" and passing "state secrets" to North Korea. However, the term "espionage" is vaguely-defined in the National Security Law and has sometimes been used to imprison people who were merely exercising their rights to freedom of expression and association. The definition of "state secrets" has included information which is publicly available in South Korea.

Long-term political prisoners are currently held in a number of different prisons throughout the country. Most are held in single cells and some have little contact with other prisoners. Conditions of imprisonment vary from prison to prison, and from prisoner to prisoner. Some prisoners appear to be in good health and are allowed to associate with other prisoners. Others are held in solitary confinement and are not allowed to mix with other prisoners. Some of the prisoners are reported to be suffering from psychological problems as a result of long-term isolation. Some suffer from digestive ailments, rheumatism, high blood pressure and other illnesses. Medical facilities in South Korean prisons are generally poor and most prisons have only one part-time doctor. Prisons are virtually unheated in winter.

Some of these prisoners are under constant pressure from the prison authorities to "convert," meaning to sign a statement renouncing their real or alleged communist views. In past decades, prisoners who refused to "convert" were often tortured. This is no longer the case today, but those who refuse are not considered for release on parole and generally have fewer rights and privileges than other prisoners. For example, visits and reading material may be restricted.

It is often difficult for long-term political prisoners to communicate with the outside world. While some are permitted to send letters to friends and supporters at home and abroad, others are not permitted to do so. While some are allowed visits from friends and supporters, others are only allowed to see close relatives. These rules sometimes appear to be applied in an arbitrary manner.

The current president, Kim Young-sam, took office in 1993 promising a new beginning with greater freedom and democracy. He is a former dissident and was the first president for several decades without a military background. In 1995, his government took an important step in addressing past human rights violations by introducing legislation to extend the statute of limitations for certain crimes, including mutiny and treason. This led to the successful prosecution of two former presidents, Roh Tae-woo and Chun Doo-hwan, and 13 other former army officials on charges that included the killings of demonstrators in Kwangju in May 1980. However,

President Kim Young-sam left many other human rights problems unresolved, including the cases of long-term political prisoners.

Although there have been a few prisoner amnesties during President Kim Young-sam's term of office, very few of the long-term political prisoners were included. Legally, there is very little possibility for these prisoners to seek redress. In South Korea, there is no independent body or individual responsible for the protection of human rights and the investigation of reported human rights violations. There has been no systematic and independent investigation into past human rights violations.

For several years, human rights lawyers and activists in South Korea have sought retrials for some long-term political prisoners as a means of obtaining redress. Under South Korea's Code of Criminal Procedure, a retrial may be granted if it is proved that evidence was forged, testimony was false and when new "clear evidence" is discovered. But the requirements for a retrial have proved to be extremely difficult to meet, and as far as Amnesty International is aware, no long-term political prisoner has secured one.

The statute of limitations on public prosecutions means it is impossible to prosecute those responsible for human rights violations inflicted on long-term political prisoners after their arrest. This is because the violations occurred too long ago for those responsible to be brought to justice under South Korean law. In January 1995, eight long-term political prisoners filed a complaint of torture against investigation officials, but their complaint was dismissed because the statute of limitations had expired.

In the absence of any legal redress for the long-term political prisoners, Amnesty International has urged the current government to find an effective remedy for these victims of human rights violations committed under previous administrations.

Amnesty International makes the following recommendations:

• *Review or release:* In some well-documented cases (including that of Kim Song-man), Amnesty International is convinced the charges against a long-term prisoner are unfounded and calls for the prisoner's immediate and unconditional release. In other cases AI is calling for a review of the cases on the grounds that the prisoners were tortured and convicted after unfair trials.

• *Investigation of past human rights violations:* Amnesty International has called on the government, the main political parties and individual legislators to seek an effective means of investigating past human rights violations. This is of particular urgency in the cases of long-term political prisoners who have already spent many years in prison.

• *Prison conditions:* Amnesty International calls on the government to ensure the conditions of imprisonment for long-term political prisoners are in conformity with international human rights standards.

Dear Bob Connelly,   12/13/95

I received your package and letter with pleasure. I ate with relish what you sent me and the ivory soap was very very useful. I am deeply grateful to you for your kind help.

Two weeks ago I moved to a new prison. It is less cold here than in the former prison and the air is fresher.

I will send you a reply to your letter soon. Now I am writing lots of Christmas cards to my friends.

I thank you from the bottom of my heart for your warm concern, help, and kindness to send me packages and letters this year.

All the happiness and special wishes to you this Christmas season.

Yours sincerely,

희망찬 새해를 맞아
가정에 웃음과 기쁨이 가득하시기를 기원합니다.

Season's Greetings and Best Wishes for the New Year

amnesty international

SOUTH KOREA

"Unconverted" Political Prisoners

July 1992
AI Index: ASA 25/15/92
Distr: SC/CO/GR

INTERNATIONAL SECRETARIAT, 1 EASTON STREET, LONDON WC1X 8DJ, UNITED KINGDOM

SOUTH KOREA
Unconverted" Political Prisoners

Amnesty International is concerned about a number of prisoners of conscience, possible prisoners of conscience and other political prisoners, convicted under national security legislation, whose continued detention appears to be a result of their refusal to renounce their real or alleged communist views. These prisoners are known as "unconverted" political prisoners, over 40 of whom have been held for some years in Taejon Prison. It is also concerned that some of the "unconverted" political prisoners may have been convicted after an unfair trial and that some may be required to renounce a communist viewpoint which they never held. It has adopted three of the "unconverted" political prisoners as prisoners of conscience and is calling for their unconditional release.

The "unconverted" political prisoners have been held for some years in Taejon Prison but according to recent reports some may now have been transferred to other prisons. They are serving lengthy prison sentences for alleged espionage activities on behalf of North Korea and the majority were convicted under previous governments. Some came from North Korea during the 1950-53 Korean War or were members of local opposition parties or resistance groups in the 1950s. Many of those arrested in later years were accused of visiting North Korea or of meeting supposed North Korean agents in Japan. Some of these prisoners claim that after their arrests they were subjected to lengthy interrogation, tortured and denied access to their families and lawyers.

The continued detention of many "unconverted" political prisoners appears to be a result of their refusal to renounce certain political beliefs. Many are serving terms of life imprisonment and some have already spent a considerable amount of time in prison. At least 30 "unconverted" political prisoners have spent more than 20 years in prison, including ten who have been held for over 30 years. Two have been in prison for over 40 years. Ordinary prisoners serving life-terms are generally released after serving between 16 and 18 years imprisonment. While other prisoners can hope to be considered for early release by the Parole Examination Board, "unconverted" prisoners are kept outside this system, a factor which is particularly acute for those serving life terms.

Amnesty International believes that some of the "unconverted" political prisoners may never have held communist beliefs or have been involved in espionage activities. It has repeatedly urged the South Korean authorities to review the cases of some "unconverted" long-term prisoners, whom it believes may have been convicted after an unfair trial. Three of the "unconverted" political prisoners, Kim Song-man, Yu Won-ho and Chang Ui-gyun, have been adopted by Amnesty International as prisoners of conscience.

Kim Song-man, a student of political science, studied in South Korea and the USA. He also travelled to several East European countries and visited the North Korean embassies in Budapest and East Berlin. He was arrested in 1985 and sentenced to life-imprisonment under the National Security Law for passing state secrets to North Koreans he met abroad and acting under their instructions. Kim Song-man denied the charges against him and said he met North Koreans to learn more about North Korea and to find out about the possibilities for reunification. Amnesty International has adopted Kim Song-man as a prisoner of conscience and is calling for his release as it does not believe there is any evidence to substantiate the charges against him. Kim Song-man has argued he should not have to "convert" because he was never involved in any spying activities. In a recent interview with his lawyer, he said:

"First of all, I believe in the principle of freedom of conscience . . . Right now, all over the world, the Cold War has ended, and even when one's ideology is different from that of others, they are still trying to seek reconciliation, so I can't agree with the proposition that I will receive special treatment only if I convert. . . ."

"The true meaning of reunification [between North and South Korea] is that people with different ideologies can freely interact and travel about in public . . . Is it true that only the government can strive for reunification? I too support reunification and cannot sign something which goes counter to reunification. I should walk freely on the street without converting . . ."

The basis for the "conversion" system is contained in a regulation issued by the Ministry of Justice in 1969. The Ministry of Justice regulation classifies political and non-political prisoners into four classes. Class A includes the prisoners who can be rehabilitated; Class B includes the prisoners whose rehabilitation is considered difficult; Class C includes prisoners whose rehabilitation is deemed very difficult, including recidivists and "prisoners of conviction" who have "converted". "Prisoners of conviction" who have not "converted" belong to Class D and are not entitled to the benefits granted in the other classes.

According to testimonies of former political prisoners, in order to show they had "converted," they were required to write a statement explaining (a) how they became Communists, (b) the activities they carried out to promote communism, (c) the reasons why they wanted to give up communism, and (d) what they proposed to do in the future. The prisoners then appeared before a committee of prison officials who decided whether to accept the statement as evidence of a true "conversion." Released political prisoners have testified that during the 1970s and 1980s many prisoners were tortured to force them to "convert." At present, however, the main pressure on prisoners is said to be a psychological one, including the denial of early release on parole. Prisoners who have not "converted" are also reportedly unable to receive and send regular correspondence, to meet visitors without guards being present, to have extra items of furniture in their cells, to work, watch television or to attend religious worship.

In February 1992 a group of "unconverted" political prisoners filed a petition with the Constitutional Court on the basis that the "conversion" system violates the rights to freedom of conscience and human dignity, guaranteed in the Constitution of the Republic of Korea.

GROUP CORRESPONDENCE

In September 1993 Group #202 received information from Clare McVey of AI's East Asia Team regarding an important decision from the United Nations Working Group on Arbitrary Detention.

Clare's letter explained that the group had been established in 1991 to examine the detention of individual prisoners, and that AI had sent a few of its cases to the group, including Kim Song-man.

In April 1993, Clare reported, the UN group determined that Kim Song-man's detention was "arbitrary" and "in contravention of various articles of the Universal Declaration of Human Rights and the International Covenant on Civil and Political Rights." She enclosed a copy of the decision for our use.

The text of the decision follows.

DECISION OF UN WORKING GROUP ON ARBITRARY DETENTION

DECISION No. 28/1993 (REPUBLIC OF KOREA)

Communication addressed to the Government of the Republic of Korea on 6 November 1992.

Concerning: Chang Ui-gyun, Hwang Tae-kwon and Kim Song-man on the one hand and the Republic of Korea on the other.

3. With a view to taking a decision the Working Group considers if the cases in question fall into one or more of the following three categories:

I. Cases in which the deprivation of freedom is arbitrary, as it manifestly cannot be linked to any legal basis (such as continued detention beyond the execution of the sentence or despite an amnesty act, etc.); or

II. Cases of deprivation of freedom when the facts giving rise to the prosecution or conviction concern *the exercise of the rights and* freedoms protected by articles 7, 13, 14, 18, 19, 20 and 21 of the Universal Declaration of Human Rights and articles 12, 18, 19, 21, 22, 25, 26 and 27 of the International-Coven I ant on Civil and Political Rights; or

III. Cases in which non-observance of all or part of the international provisions relating to the right to a fair trial is such that it confers on the deprivation of freedom, of whatever kind, an arbitrary character.

12. In the light of the above the Working Group decides:

The detention of Chang Ui-gyun, Hwang Tae-kwon and Kim Song-man is declared to be arbitrary being in contravention of articles 5, 9, 19 and 21 of the Universal Declaration of Human Rights, and articles 7, 9, 14, 19 and 21 of the International Covenant on Civil. and Political Rights and falling within categories II and III of the principles applicable in the consideration of the cases submitted to the Working Group.

Adopted on 30 April 1993.

Kim Song-man was one of the prisoners featured to receive holiday cards in 1995.

Send the Gift of Hope

Holiday Card Action
1995

Each year during the winter holidays, Amnesty International asks friends and members to send greeting cards to those who have suffered human rights violations.

Holidays mean little to prisoners who believe they have been forgotten by the world. A simple greeting card, however, can bring renewed hope. You can let those featured on the following pages know that they are not forgotten. When sending your cards:

♪ Remember that simple messages of goodwill and greeting are enough. Do not discuss politics or accusations directed against the prisoners.

♪ Do not mention Amnesty International or use AI greeting cards. To do so lessens the likelihood that your cards will reach the prisoner and could negatively affect her or his situation.

♪ Since these individuals hold diverse religious beliefs, please do not send Christmas or other religious-themed cards. Also, please note that references to alcoholic beverages (for example, a champagne bottle pictured on a New Year's card) could be offensive in some cultures.

♪ Cards may be sent until January 31, 1996.

Amnesty International USA

KOREA AND JAPAN
REGIONAL ACTION NETWORK

A message from Amnesty International's East Asia Team in May 1997 described a planned event by 16 human rights organizations in South Korea. The action was scheduled for August 7 - 9, 1997 to call attention to the prisoners of conscience and to urge their release. The organizers also wished to use the opportunity to call for an investigation of past human rights violations.

Amnesty International urged members to send messages of support to the South Korean activists, and to send clippings about group campaign efforts in South Korea.

The timing was intended to coincide with the anniversary of Korea's freedom from Japanese colonial rule. In 1997, nearly 300 arrests were made under the National Security Law (the same law used to charge Kim Song-man). The organizers of the event sought to highlight the human rights violations committed under two former presidents, Chun Doo-hwan and Roh Tae-woo. Both men were in prison at the time on charges of corruption and human rights violations, but the groups feared that they would be officially pardoned.

Peaceful demonstrations and numerous "street acts," a "night of hope" for prisoners of conscience, and exhibitions of letters and other testimonials from around the world were planned.

The Minkahyup human rights group was the principal sponsor with support from Lawyers for Democracy; Korean Confederation of Trade Unions; Korean Professors Association for Democracy; National Council of Churches in Korea; Catholic Human Rights Committee; Citizens Coalition for Economic Justice; Sarangbang human rights centre; Korean Women's' Associations United; National Association of Buddhist Monks; Korean Association of Anglican Priests for Justice; People's Solidarity for Participatory Democracy; Association of Physicians for Humanism.

Amnesty International's show of support for such activities helps encourage human rights groups in their important work around the world.